Modern Critical Interpretations
# Aeschylus's
# The Oresteia

# Modern Critical Interpretations

*These and other titles in preparation*

*Modern Critical Interpretations*

Aeschylus's

# The Oresteia

*Edited and with an introduction by*

Harold Bloom
*Sterling Professor of the Humanities*
*Yale University*

*Chelsea House Publishers* ◊ *1988*

NEW YORK ◊ NEW HAVEN ◊ PHILADELPHIA

882.01
A

21 July 88 Gum Drop Ten.

© 1988 by Chelsea House Publishers, a division
of Chelsea House Educational Communications, Inc.,
  345 Whitney Avenue, New Haven, CT 06511
  95 Madison Avenue, New York, NY 10016
  5068B West Chester Pike, Edgemont, PA 19028

Introduction © 1988 by Harold Bloom

Printed and bound in the United States of America

10  9  8  7  6  5  4  3  2  1

∞ The paper used in this publication meets the minimum
requirements of the American National Standard for Permanence
of Paper for Printed Library Materials, Z39.48–1984.

Library of Congress Cataloging-in-Publication Data
Aeschylus's Oresteia / edited and with an introduction by Harold
Bloom.
  p.  cm.—(Modern critical interpretations.)
  Bibliography: p.
  Includes index.
  ISBN 0–87754–903–6 (alk. paper) : $24.50
  1. Aeschylus. Oresteia.  2. Orestes (Greek mythology) in
literature.  I. Bloom, Harold.  II. Aeschylus. Oresteia.
III. Series.
PA3825.A6A37  1988
882'.01—dc19                                                                87–18343
                                                              CIP

# Contents

# Editor's Note

This book brings together a representative selection of the best modern critical interpretations of the *Oresteia* of Aeschylus. The critical essays are reprinted here in the chronological order of their original publication. I am grateful to Douglas Smith for his assistance in editing this volume.

My introduction centers upon Clytemnestra as a figure of negative sublimity, imaginatively stronger than either Agamemnon or Orestes. John Jones begins the chronological sequence of criticism with his meditation upon the thematic cluster he calls the drama's "corporate fight for health and life, and the single great death threatening all."

In Anne Lebeck's study of the *Libation-Bearers,* we are led to the conclusion that "Orestes truly is his mother's own." Froma I. Zeitlin, analyzing what she terms "the dynamics of misogyny" in the *Oresteia,* views Athena as the "truly positive female figure" in the trilogy.

Hunting and sacrifice are expounded by Pierre Vidal-Naquet as interlocked and crucial themes in the *Oresteia.* The tragic emotions are contextualized by W. B. Stanford, in a close study of the emotive methods used by a master poet, as leading up to the happiest and most optimistic ending in all of Greek tragedy.

In this volume's concluding essay, John Herington imaginatively brings together the many elements that constitute the poetry of Aeschylus and that allow it so triumphantly to represent its "no-man's-land of dark and light," one of the most superb instances of a visionary cosmos in Western literature.

# Introduction

Agamemnon, Orestes, and Electra are all of them strong characters, but readers or playgoers confronting *Agamemnon* and the *Libation-Bearers* are likeliest to remember Clytemnestra. She has a savage inwardness that is different in kind, not just in degree, from the consciousness of the other survivors in her immediate family. Aeschylus is not much interested in psychology, according to many of his scholars, and Agamemnon has little in him that resembles the probing intensity of the Oedipus of Sophocles or even the Orestes of Euripides. Like his contemporary, Pindar, Aeschylus sometimes can seem closer to the archaic view of man than to the Sophoclean. His Agamemnon is a smaller figure necessarily than the war-leader of the *Iliad,* but the deep similarities are undeniable. The largest difference is the background or context, which is so menacing in Aeschylus as to diminish his protagonists, except again for Clytemnestra. When I read the *Oresteia,* I receive the uncanny impression that Aeschylus somehow precedes Homer in time, if only because the cosmos and the gods seem more archaic, less rational even than they do in the *Iliad.*

In the cosmos with Aeschylus, there is always choice or will, but essentially it is a choice between catastrophes. Homer's world is dangerous, but you can choose a right way, within the limits of the gods' designs upon you. The *Oresteia* shows you great figures caught between wrong and wrong, or between the daemonic and the divine, where the two are ambiguously mixed. Some scholars attribute this to the curse upon the house of Atreus, but the ambiguity is present in Aeschylus elsewhere. E. R. Dodds, in his *The Greeks and the Irrational,* sees the movement from Homer to Aeschylus as being from shame-culture to guilt-culture. Yet guilt is so endemic in the *Oresteia* that it seems more than cultural, seems reality itself. Aeschylus is so difficult a poet for us because either we must assimilate his sense of guilt to paradigms we can comprehend—

1

Christian or Freudian—or else acknowledge that the *Oresteia* is somehow more remote from us than even the *Iliad* now is.

One way in which the flamboyant Clytemnestra refreshes us is that we do not have to debate just how guilty she is. There are ambiguities in the guilt of Agamemnon and the guilt of Orestes, but Clytemnestra is gloriously culpable, overtly exultant at having butchered Agamemnon and poor Cassandra:

> CLYTEMNESTRA: Now hear you this, the right behind my sacrament:
> By my child's Justice driven to fulfilment, by
> her Wrath and Fury, to whom I sacrificed this man,
> the hope that walks my chambers is not traced with fear
> while yet Aegisthus makes the fire shine on my hearth,
> my good friend, now as always, who shall be for us
> the shield of our defiance, no weak thing; while he,
> this other, is fallen, stained with this woman you behold,
> plaything of all the golden girls at Ilium;
> and here lies she, the captive of his spear, who saw
> wonders, who shared his bed, the wise in revelations
> and loving mistress, who yet knew the feel as well
> of the men's rowing benches. Their reward is not
> unworthy. He lies there; and she who swanlike cried
> aloud her lyric mortal lamentation out
> is laid against his fond heart, and to me has given
> a delicate excitement to my bed's delight.

The "sacrament" is murder, the "sacrifice" a vengeance for the sacrifice of Iphigeneia, but the gratuitous horror is the enormous relish with which Clytemnestra rejoices in her murder of Cassandra, a rejoicing that achieves an apotheosis in erotic sadism: "and to me has given / a delicate excitement to my bed's delight." Is there a comparable figure to Clytemnestra in Homer? Her sister Helen is the only possibility, and fades rapidly juxtaposed to Agamemnon's fatal wife, who is a personage of sinister authority. Her hatred of her husband has a sexual element in it, a resentment of a ruler weaker and less cunning than herself, who takes precedence over her only because he is a male.

Clytemnestra is most herself as a personage precisely where Aeschylus is most himself as a poet, in the crimson path of tapestries Agamemnon walks upon to his slaughter. For Clytemnestra, it is the emblem of the triumph of her will over his; for Aeschylus it is one with his motive for metaphor, with the will to representation that drives him to write his plays. Few acts of the ancient imagination are as superbly memorable as Clytemnestra's association of the trodden tapestries with the rich robes by which she has netted the king:

CLYTEMNESTRA: Much have I said before to serve necessity,
  but I will take no shame now to unsay it all.
  How else could I, arming hate against hateful men
  disguised in seeming tenderness, fence high the nets
  of ruin beyond overleaping? Thus to me
  the conflict born of ancient bitterness is not
  a thing new thought upon, but pondered deep in time.
  I stand now where I struck him down. The thing is done.
  Thus have I wrought, and I will not deny it now.
  That he might not escape nor beat aside his death,
  as fishermen cast their huge circling nets, I spread
  deadly abundance of rich robes, and caught him fast.
  I struck him twice. In two great cries of agony
  he buckled at the knees and fell. When he was down
  I struck him the third blow, in thanks and reverence
  to Zeus the lord of dead men underneath the ground.
  Thus he went down, and the life struggled out of him;
  and as he died he spattered me with the dark red
  and violent driven rain of bitter savored blood
  to make me glad, as gardens stand among the showers
  of God in glory at the birthtime of the buds.

  These being the facts, elders of Argos assembled here,
  be glad, if it be your pleasure; but for me, I glory.
  Were it religion to pour wine above the slain,
  this man deserved, more than deserved, such sacrament.
  He filled our cup with evil things unspeakable
  and now himself come home has drunk it to the dregs.

This astonishing declaration is so powerful that its full implications require almost endless meditation. Clytemnestra's pride in her deed is absolute, and ensues from a hatred so transcendent that it embraces Zeus as another representative of male sexuality, which is her true victim. The blood of Agamemnon substitutes for his semen, and her glad glory is nourished by that life's blood. So long-meditated a revenge has about it a peculiar guilt, yet Clytemnestra has joined a beyond, a negative sublime that cannot be touched by guilt. Her last words, spoken to Orestes before he takes her within the house to her death, are defiant and angry, and again directed against maleness: "You are the snake I gave birth to, and gave the breast."

It is difficult to believe that Aeschylus could have intended the rhetorical, indeed poetic triumph that Clytemnestra wins over both Agamemnon and Orestes. But father and son, though very different, are flawed, guilt-driven, doom-eager yet lacking in color, nerve, even in eloquence. Clytemnestra keeps her hold upon the imagination, and is prophetic of much that has come to us, and more that may come. She excites no sympathy, yet her originality and force are undiminished. Her strength is that guilt and shame alike are alien to her. Aeschylus possessed a greater insight into the darkness of the war between men and women than any other dramatist before Shakespeare. Clytemnestra's ghost inhabits that darkness, and goes on calling to the sleeping Furies: "Up, let not work's weariness / beat you, nor slacken with sleep so you forget my pain."

# The House of Atreus

*John Jones*

A watchman lies stretched out on the roof of Agamemnon's palace, propped on his elbows, scanning the horizon for the prearranged beacon-fire which will announce the capture of Troy. The physical and visible situation delivers the *Oresteia*'s opening complete, full-formed; it were an absurd inadequacy to speak of this disposition as having dramatic point. The watchman lying on top of the building (represented by the permanent *skēnē* before which the action takes place) is the eye and tongue and consciousness of the household asleep beneath him, and the poet's means of communicating its mood. "I weep," he says, recounting his weary watch,

> and I groan over the troubles of this house of ours, no longer ordered for the best as it once was. And tonight I pray for a happy release from my task: may the beacon-fire carry its glad news through the darkness.
>
> *(Agamemnon, ll. 18–21)*

And at that moment, in a congruence of wish and fact found throughout Greek tragedy, the fire burns up in the distance. He rouses the palace:

> Hullo! Hullo then! This loud cry of mine gives Agamemnon's wife the signal to rise from her couch with all speed and send a shout of thankful joy ringing through the house, in welcome to this fire.
>
> *(ll. 25–29)*

From *On Aristotle and Greek Tragedy*. © 1962 by John Jones. Chatto & Windus Ltd., 1962.

And his speech ends with a sudden shift from joy at Troy's capture to anxious concern for the house and its affairs:

> Ah well, may he come home, the master of our house; and
> may I hold his dear hand in mine. But for the rest—I'm dumb:
> a great ox is standing on my tongue. And yet the house itself,
> could it but speak, would have a plain tale to tell.
>
> (ll. 34–38)

This short opening scene gets across to the audience (in a world without theatre programmes) necessary background information as to the time and place and people of the action, and it also asserts an intense, unremitting focus on the "house," the fortunes of which will be followed through the play and through the trilogy, into the next generation. The note of tragic disquiet in the watchman's speech issues from the house (observe the delicate and arrested movement towards personification in "the house itself, could it but speak") and concerns itself; the human individuals are apprehended only in relation to the household which contains them—not merely the watchman-servant perched up there on the roof for everyone to see, but those chief people of the story to whom he refers: the absent king is not "Agamemnon" but "the master of the house," his queen is not "Clytemnestra" but "Agamemnon's wife"—both of them designated by their household status and function. "House" (the Greek *oikos* and its synonyms) is at once house and household, building and family, land and chattels, slaves and domestic animals, hearth and ancestral grave: a psycho-physical community of the living and the dead and the unborn. The master of the house is priest in charge of the family cult (in which slaves attached to the *oikos* participate) as well as its secular head, and his wife is bound to him through the *oikos* which she joins at marriage. Marriage is not primarily a business of personal relations—still less of romantic love—but of securing the continuity of the *oikos*.

Aeschylus's first audience will have been more receptive than we can hope to be of the image of this *oikos*—the house of Atreus—which the watchman establishes. For us it is a conscious but necessary effort to accept this image for what it is, and to retain it while the watchman descends and disappears from sight, and the Chorus file into the *orchēstra* and sing their opening song. They narrate the mustering of the expedition to punish Paris and his city, the anger of Artemis and Agamemnon's sacrifice of Iphigeneia; and as they are finishing their song Clytemnestra enters to give them the news of Troy's capture. There follows a long dialogue between queen and Chorus, at the end of which, in the second choral song, credit for the Greek victory is given to Zeus and just retribution is held to have visited Paris "who entered the house of the sons of Atreus and dishonoured his hosts' table by stealing the wife away" (ll. 399–402).

The plural "sons of Atreus" is remarkable. Aeschylus has altered the traditional form of the story (and violated the laws of human probability as the Greeks understood them) by making Agamemnon and Menelaus share a house. By this deviation he gives Agamemnon a claim against Paris alongside that of his brother, Helen's husband, and—more important than the legal issue—he avoids the dissipation of interest that would result if the web of action and reaction, crime and retribution, were extended beyond the one *oikos* which he wishes to keep in the dramatic foreground throughout. Still greater concentration is achieved by disposing of the Trojan war before Agamemnon returns. The herald, arriving ahead of his king, delivers an extended quasi-epic narrative of the fighting and its hardships; and now the time is ripe for Agamemnon's entry. The war is a dying theme, and an extreme simplicity of situation prevails. We are witnessing a homecoming.

Agamemnon greets his country and his country's gods, proclaims that he will appoint assemblies to consider matters of state and public worship, and concludes:

> And now I will enter my palace and approach my household
> hearth, first of all saluting the gods who sped me forth and
> have brought me home. Victory has attended me; may she stay
> with me always.
>
> (ll. 851–54)

No word of Clytemnestra. The focus is the *focus*—the socio-religious hearth of Indo-European societies and a living force to Aeschylus and his audience—now to be approached after long absence by the household's master who is also its priest. To feel the moment in this way is the first step toward a just reading of the carpet scene. The carpet lies between Agamemnon and his hearth: this is the situation which commentators have obscured in two closely related ways, by psychologising the meeting of husband and wife into a process of temptation, and by spiritualising a quarrel about treading upon a carpet into something supposedly more exalted. Their joint effect is to reduce the carpet to a physical pawn in a mental conflict.

When Clytemnestra's women have strewn the purple tapestries in front of him, Agamemnon declares that he will not be pampered like a woman or grovelled to like a barbarian king:

> And do not draw down Envy upon my path by strewing it with tapestries. Such honours are for gods; I think with dread of a mortal man treading on fine embroidered work. Pay me the respect due a man, not a god.
>
> (ll. 921–25)

Mortal hubris and divine jealousy or envy (*phthonos*) are here, as so often, interlocked. And when Agamemnon says that to tread on the tapestries would be an act of insolent pride and folly likely to incur retribution from above, it is important to recognise that he is shrinking from something wider than almost any modern formulation of impiety. Hubris embraces the familiar impieties as an offshoot of its wide-branching central meaning of doing deeds and thinking thoughts "greater" than those which a human being ought to do and think. Everywhere in Greek tragedy we find hubris, and the fear of hubris, arising in contexts which are not obviously religious; and in the carpet scene our sense of impiety should be muted to the point of integration within this broad ancient concept: in fact it is a mistake to think of the tapestries as dedicated to religious uses, because we shall thus be led into the false precision that conceives of Clytemnestra urging Agamemnon to commit an act of clear-cut sacrilege. Faced with the tapestries, Agamemnon says it would ill become a human being to tread on them. Why? He suggests the answer himself: "I think with dread of a mortal man treading on fine embroidered work." The tapestries are precious; a lot of work has gone into them. No further reason is offered in the course of the ensuing dialogue (it is said that people in general will disapprove, which merely leads us to ask why they should) until, at last, Agamemnon suddenly yields:

> Well, if you will have it so—let someone undo my shoes, and quickly. . . . And may no god glance malignly on me from afar as I tread upon these purple dyes. It awakes the deepest shame, this wasting of our house's substance with my feet and spoiling of costly woven fabrics.
>
> (ll. 944–49)

The suggestion contained in "fine embroidered work" is now fully explicit; Agamemnon's initial rebuke to Clytemnestra was rooted in his unwillingness to waste the substance of the *oikos*. His "pay me the respect due a man, not a god" was directed to the truth that it would be fitting for a god to be offered some element of the household's wealth (this is of course the point of sacrificial destruction of objects), but to address that kind of service to a man could only result in a wanton wounding of the body of the house. One must be ready, and glad, to admit a certain largeness of poetic treatment. Aeschylus is not pressing upon us the thought of tapestries being sacrificed to gods. He is concentrating on the destruction of *oikos*-substance, and distinguishing the kinds of respect proper towards gods and towards men. (A near-absurdity arises when we stress, as I believe all commentators have done, the narrow transgression of walking on the tapestries rather than the broad hubris of wasting the house's wealth: we find ourselves regarding the tapestries as somehow reserved for the feet of gods. Indeed Agamemnon himself admits, according to the better interpretation of the controversial lines 931–34, that for a man to walk upon tapestries like the ones now in his path is not necessarily an impious action.)

And again, while a servant is taking off his shoes—a gesture of modesty and of respect for the precious stuff, and also an attempt to minimise damage—Agamemnon declares his fear of divine *phthonos* ("may no god glance malignly on me"), now in direct association with the religious "shame" (*aidōs*) of the wealth-wasting. And he sets foot on the tapestries. And thus his homecoming is a harming of his house, the lucid externality of this equivalence presenting a complete and painful dramatic sense: the thing is done, it shows itself.

If any doubt remains as to where interpretative emphasis should rest, it is dispelled by Clytemnestra's words at the moment when Agamemnon gives way to her:

> The sea—who shall drain the sea?—is at hand with its store
> of purple stain for dyeing fine things, abundant, precious as
> silver, eternally renewed. And of fine things, my king, there
> is no lack in our house—by the god's grace: our house does
> not know how to be poor. I would have devoted many such
> to be trodden underfoot, if some oracle had required this trib-
> ute of the house when I was casting about for means to secure
> your safe return.
>
> (ll. 958–65)

She directs her attention (as, from behind her, Aeschylus directs ours) towards the household's wealth; she counters her husband's scruples with the argument that the *oikos* can afford the waste that is taking place at this moment, as Agamemnon walks along the tapestries into the palace.

The religious fear which prompted his rebuke of Clytemnestra and his initial refusal to tread on the tapestries now moves into the dramatic foreground, for Clytemnestra's sentiment that the *oikos* is so rich that it need not bother about this kind of extravagance, while trivial-seeming to us, will have struck a fifth-century audience as recklessly hubristic; and they will have observed a vital distinction between the senseless wantonness taking place in front of them and the hypothetical circumstances envisaged by Clytemnestra of the same destruction following an oracle's command. Great wealth linked with high station had been from early times the subject of moral reflection on the virtues of moderation and restraint. Eminence did not arouse in the Greeks a narrow hostility or envy, but it did seem to them singularly vulnerable; they never tired of saying, in their tragic literature and elsewhere, that to be prominent and prosperous and at the same time to avoid hubris is exquisitely difficult. The old men of the *Agamemnon*'s Chorus show a timidity and eagerness for a life obscure enough to escape heaven's jealous eye which one might parallel in almost any extant Greek tragedy. Nevertheless, the choral songs of this play are exceptional in the degree to which they isolate and dwell upon material prosperity. I am saying that the great tragic subject of Excess is being given economic point.

An important function of choral meditation is to create and sustain atmosphere, to foster thematic affinities. Early in the play, after Clytemnestra has told them of Troy's capture, they reflect:

> Disaster, the child of reckless folly, is with us for all to see, when the house of the proud-hearted is crammed with wealth in excess, beyond what is best. Our prayer is for sufficiency without sorrow, for that share which the wise man calls enough. There is no escape for him who, wanton in his wealth, thrusts the exalted seat of Justice out of sight, out of mind.
>
> (ll. 374–84)

Their burden is Paris's guilt and just punishment, but the link between his abduction of Helen and their large moralising upon riches is extremely tenuous—although we ought not to forget that Paris has enriched his household and his city by this theft. Aeschylus is availing himself of the opportunity given in the Chorus's lyrical elaborations—the intrusive author's voice of Victorian fiction achieves a similar end more blatantly—to provide reader and spectator with an ultimate objectivity of reference, like a key signature. This reaches us as a religio-moral drift in which the action is suspended. When he gives the following passage to the Chorus at the long-awaited moment of Agamemnon's entry:

> Justice sets store by a righteous life, and her light shines in the smoky dwellings of the poor. But she departs with averted eyes from gold-encrusted halls where men's hands are defiled, taking her way to innocent homes. She does not bow to the power of wealth stamped false with idle praise; she guides all things to their fulfilment.
>
> Hail, my King, stormer of Troy, Atreus's son.
>
> (ll. 773–81)

It is no accident that Agamemnon appears when he does: but this is not to say that the words are directed at him in the form of personal indictment. Indeed they are not directed *at* him at all; we must allow the theme of unholy wealth and the visible figure of the king simply to coexist in our reception of the scene. The Chorus's remarks are suitably general in tone since their application is collective. They anticipate the self-wounding of the *oikos* which is soon to be presented in the spoiling of the tapestries.

Aeschylus has thus made careful preparation for the carpet scene, to insure that its sense shall not be misapprehended. Nor can one doubt the hubris entailed in Clytemnestra's defending of waste by an appeal to wealth; the Chorus's religio-moral brooding has produced a state of attentiveness in which doubt is impossible. Furthermore, the choral song which follows her speech contains an indirect refutation of its argument:

> The ship of human fortune, holding a straight course onward, strikes a hidden reef. Then, if a well-judged heave tips part of the cargo overboard, the wisely fearful captain saves his ship from foundering: and a house too, no longer over-freighted, escapes total wreck.
>
> (ll. 1005–13)

The *oikos*—any *oikos*—is being likened in a forcefully collective quasi-simile (the likeness sliding characteristically toward identification) to a ship at sea, and the Chorus is envisaging circumstances in which it would be a blameless and prudent decision to sacrifice part of the corporate wealth in order to save the rest. A comparison between purposeful surrender and purposeless waste emerges into consciousness almost unprompted. Clytemnestra is not directly challenged, but the economic bias of her hubris cannot be overlooked. We have noted a similar oblique commentary investing Agamemnon; the Chorus's words immediately before his entry are not directed at him, but they are felt to have been thrown round him; and when, in the song which comes to an end with his dying cry, they affirm: "Mankind never has its fill of prosperity" (ll. 1331–32)—an unattached piece of moralising, even by the standards of Greek tragedy—one experiences an *oikos*-focussed rightness of context which occupies the place both of causation (Agamemnon isn't killed because he walked on the tapestries) and of personal justice (he doesn't deserve to die for walking on the tapestries). Likewise when Clytemnestra turns to Cassandra, the captive Trojan seer whom Agamemnon has brought home with him, and orders her to go inside the house and take her stand "with many another slave at the altar of the god who guards its wealth," adding that she has "reason to be deeply thankful for having masters old in wealth" (ll. 1037–38, 1043), the bitterness of Cassandra's situation (she is being sent inside to be murdered, which she knows through her seer's gift but cannot prevent) stands in the kind of relation we are considering—thematically pointed but causally remote—to the hubris of her new mistress.

I am not trying to subordinate Agamemnon's murder to the carpet scene, but to understand both in the light of Aeschylus's intention to dramatise the troubles of the house of Atreus. The point of immediate relevance is the dwarfing of all other consideration by the corporate consequences of these two outrages committed within the *oikos*, against itself. The Chorus's response to Agamemnon's death-cry is public and institutional; they talk of "a plot to set up a tyranny in the city" on the part of the two "defilers of the house" ("murderers" would be too narrow a designation of those who have killed the king and master of the *oikos*), and when Clytemnestra appears before them to justify her action they reply to her with waverings and contrapuntal blendings of opinion, blaming her, admitting Agamemnon's guilt, confessing themselves unable to judge between the adversaries; but the dominant strain is their dismay, which is the corporate dismay of the stricken *oikos*:

> I am at a loss what to think and where to turn, now the house
> is tottering; I fear the pelting storm of blood that shakes the
> house,
>
> (ll. 1530–34)

and their horror of the evil spirit (*daimōn*) which has been seen through successive generations of the house of Atreus, and which is now at work again. The potency of the family *daimōn* and its central place in the trilogy is shown in the way it unites accusers and accused in a search for some means of appeasement: the Chorus and Clytemnestra in this play; Orestes, Electra, Clytemnestra, and the Chorus of household slave-women in the next; the parties to the judicial proceedings in the last. Even more terrible is its power of lending opposed individuals a deeper harmony in wrongdoing; when Agamemnon is walking along the tapestries and Clytemnestra is saying there are plenty more where those came from, the greatness of the scene touches us through our haunting awareness of conspiracy. The *daimōn* is felt by all, and presented by Aeschylus, as bigger than the human beings; we should not take Clytemnestra's assertion that the "evil genius of Atreus" assumed her shape in order to kill Agamemnon merely on the plane of self-excuse. The Chorus, who are not her friends, see more in it than that. They refuse to believe that she had no part in the murder, but they admit "a spirit of vengeance, provoked by his father's crime, might help you in this" (ll. 1507–8). The shadow of the family *daimōn* falls across the generations and across the whole of this long dialogue, most darkly in the speech of Clytemnestra which closes it:

> This is the covenant which I, for my part, am ready to make
> with the *daimōn* of the house of Pleisthenes: I will accept—not
> an easy thing for me—all that has been done and suffered, if
> from now on he will leave our house and drag down some
> other family by kinsmen's murdering of kinsmen. I shall be
> content with a small part of the household wealth, once I have
> rid this palace of the madness of family bloodshed.
>
> (ll. 1568–76)

The *daimōn* is a persecuting quasi-physical presence which Clytemnestra hopes to divert from the house of Atreus towards another family—it doesn't matter which. And she hopes to achieve her object by buying the *daimōn* off. Now, near the end of the *Agamemnon,* the apparently disparate themes of economic hubris and the family *daimōn* draw close together. There is nothing unnatural or violent in this, because Aeschylus's *daimōn* spreads beyond the exclusive spirituality of our "hereditary guilt," while his *oikos*-substance, unlike our "wealth," does not feel the tug of a gravitational materiality. On the one hand, guilt is or is not extinguished; it cannot be diverted, as Clytemnestra plans to divert the *daimōn.* On the other, goods and money are not material objects attaching to the *oikos;* they inhere in its psycho-physical body. We therefore find the (for us) tired metaphor of unholy wealth exerting an immediate literal force throughout the *Oresteia*. Unholy wealth is more than unjustly acquired wealth; it is wealth which has lost its virtue and efficacy, described by the Chorus in a passage already quoted as "wealth stamped false with idle praise"—seeming-wealth, a counterfeit, not real wealth at all. And so the principal conclusion to be drawn from Clytemnestra's speech, in the light of choral commentary and subsequent event, is not that the *daimōn* cannot be bribed but that she has nothing to bribe it with. Once the situation is seen in terms of the internal relations of the *oikos,* and once we cease to force on Aeschylus a rigid separation of physical and mental, the tragic futility becomes evident of Clytemnestra's plan to appease the family *daimōn* by offering it the defiled and reduced substance of the family: stress upon her plan being lighter than upon the family's helplessness.

The family's privation demonstrates its guilt, and its guilt is scarcely touched upon in the personalistic debate about Agamemnon's deserving in relation to his murder. The vagaries, contradictions and obscurities which (we saw) frustrate the search for an intelligible, and not merely for an acceptable, morality or rationale of guilt and innocence, are not there for Aeschylus because Agamemnon himself—the Agamemnon of the critics, the autonomous, self-sustaining modern man—is not there. Aeschylus's Agamemnon draws his life, and with his life his guilts and innocences, from the *oikos:* "when a house is righteous the lot of its children is blessed for ever" (ll. 761–62) is the truth. The converse also holds, and no protest of outraged individuality follows the receiving of guilt from outside. Why should it? Life is fostered and transmitted by the *oikos* (the *oikos* contains the individual because it sustains him—not because of any social doctrine to that effect), so there can be no thought of sealing oneself off from whatever flows suspended in life's stream.

Vagueness in presenting guilt and the absence of the outraged individual are dramatically intrinsicate. No need asserts itself, or desire, to be precise about guilt when guilt is circumambient, atmospheric, bloodborne, often untethered to personal act or omission; where in the nature of things there can be no knowing how a man stands with his gods. The palpitating unease of Greek tragedy springs from a world in which to be sure your hands are clean is to convict yourself of hubris. In the *Oresteia,* Aeschylus dramatises this large aspect of his society's *Weltanschauung* by investing the house of Atreus with a murky, incompletely comprehended web of religio-legal culpability, and by making the chain reaction of crime and fresh crime recede into a totally obscure past. It is repeatedly stated, with varied inflection, that Agamemnon's father tricked his brother

Thyestes into eating his own children; but we also learn from Cassandra that Atreus's action was not unprovoked: Thyestes had committed adultery with his brother's wife. Cassandra also speaks of a "primal sin" lying at the root of present calamities, but she does not specify its nature. The resulting disagreement among scholars (some refer her words to Thyestes' adultery, others to even more remote crimes within the family) in their attempts to remove this doubt does homage to Aeschylus's achievement in weaving round the body of the *oikos* a seamless garment of sin-begotten and sin-begetting action in which the individual threads lose themselves within the whole. Family guilt is as much collective as inherited, in that the dead of the group form one enduring community with the living; both are prominent in the *Oresteia,* and both are fully endorsed by Aeschylus. The final settlement of the *Eumenides* expressly upholds the Furies' right to pursue a man for his ancestor's wrongdoing: "It is the sins of bygone generations that bring him before them for judgment, and Destruction strikes him down—silently, in dreadful wrath."

The morality of the *Oresteia*—moralising in a vacuum has been the special vice of Anglo-Saxon commentators—is one with the great arc which its action describes, from the watchman perched on the palace roof to the acquitted Orestes whose response to deliverance from the Furies is a corporate thanksgiving: "O Pallas, O saviour of my house!"—ample and lively enough to carry the individual's gratitude. We have paused over the murder of Agamemnon to indicate the gross distortion caused by the severance of morality from *oikos*-focussed action in an attempt to make it serve the king's single fate. It remains to say that the genuine moral chaos which ensues is less unfortunate than the false dramatic clarity of a climactic death in which the two defilers of the house become murderers above all else, and in which the vital pulse of the trilogy is lost. As the self-wounding of the house in the carpet scene moves towards the cutting off of its head, so the cutting off of its head moves towards the *de facto* transfer of authority which gives the close of the *Agamemnon* its subtle questioning lift. "I and thou," Clytemnestra tells Aegisthus, "ruling this house together, will make all well" (ll. 1672–73). How? We recall her plan to buy off the family *daimōn.* Aegisthus's assertion: "I shall try to control the people with his [Agamemnon's] wealth" (ll. 1638–39) accompanies the economic hubris of his more important partner and helps define the openness of the ending. The two lovers are no less deeply committed to the house of Atreus than was its master whom they have just killed. When the Chorus threaten Clytemnestra with reprisals after the murder, she answers, untranslatably: "For me, Hope does not set foot within the house of Fear so long as the fire upon my hearth is kindled by Aegisthus" (ll. 1434–36), thus throwing herself on his protection, not in virtue of the personal and erotic relation between them, but of his socio-religious headship of the *oikos,* as she hopes to see it asserted and maintained. But Aegisthus's task is impossible; in the same sense that unholy wealth is a false appearance of wealth, the household hearth tended by the usurper remains cold. We have already seen enough to know that the seizure of authority initiated through Agamemnon's murder is but part of a larger and as yet undetermined whole. This settlement is shallow-rooted: "the house is tottering."

The means of salvation for the self-tormented *oikos* is hinted in the *Agamemnon* by the passing mention of Orestes. We learn he has been sent away during Agamemnon's absence to the house of a friendly prince; Cassandra has a prophetic vision of Clytemnestra's death at her son's hand, and the Chorus express the hope, very near the end of the play, that a superhuman power "guiding Orestes shall bring him home again." Orestes is both of the house, being son to the murdered king, and at the same time no party to the action of the first play of the trilogy, being then absent and a child. He is singled out by blood and status for the task of restoration, and when the *Libation-Bearers* opens with the arrival of Orestes from abroad at Agamemnon's tomb, near the palace, we are witnessing the return of hope—of "the eye of the house" as the Chorus of domestic slave-women call him, its leading and most precious faculty.

The story of the *Libation-Bearers* is Orestes' fulfilment of his mission, and it is important to understand what this mission is. Too much emphasis, in the prevailing critical tradition, has been placed on Orestes' duty to avenge his father: this is a continuance of the spiritualised and personalistic interpretation which we have noted in the *Agamemnon,* and the kind of damage which results is similar. Just as Agamemnon's murder falls within a context of transfer (or attempted transfer) of authority within the *oikos,* so the retributive killing of Clytemnestra must be referred to a larger scheme of corporate restitution and amendment. The Chorus of the *Agamemnon* threaten Clytemnestra with exile and Aegisthus with death by stoning—punishments inflicted by the community for an offence against itself and peculiarly noxious to itself. The Chorus of the *Libation-Bearers* welcome Orestes as the restorer of health to this same community; the self-wounding of the *oikos* presented in the *Agamemnon* is followed after many years by its self-healing:

The house has a cure to heal these troubles: not from outside,
at alien hands, but from itself.

(ll. 471–73)

On his return, Orestes finds his sister Electra in helpless subjection
to the tyranny of Clytemnestra and Aegisthus, but passively allied with
the Chorus through "the common hatred we are nursing within the
house." They lament the pollution of the hearth—the household's altar
and centre of its corporate life—and the long drawn out wasting of
wealth; and when Orestes has made himself known, the Chorus anticipate the result of his encounter with their enemies by extending to him
and his sister—the one who watched and hated as well as the one who
is about to act—the very broad title of "saviours of your father's hearth."

No murdered father's ghost appears in the *Libation-Bearers,* to speak
and be seen, to cry Revenge, like old Hamlet. But Agamemnon's spirit
is believed to haunt his tomb, and Orestes and Electra both pray to it,
asking for help and intensifying the "common hatred" which is as yet
their only weapon. The object of the following savage exchange:

ORESTES: Father, remember the bath which gave your murderers their moment.

ELECTRA: Remember the cloak—the strange casting-net they
devised for you.

ORESTES: They shackled you, my father, with fetters of thread,
not metal-forged.

ELECTRA: They wound about you a wrapping shamefully con-
trived.

ORESTES: Father, are you not roused by these taunts of ours?

(ll. 491–95)

is to achieve even greater psychic concentration against the two defilers
and wasters of wealth: the revenge-motif, insofar as we may formally
distinguish it, serves the group's solidarity in hating. And fostering the
hatred of the group is itself ancillary to demonstrating the group's unity
in fact, its single interest. Orestes and Electra pray to Agamemnon:

ELECTRA: Listen, father, to this last cry; look on us your children crouched before your tomb; and pity us both, the
woman and the man too.

ORESTES: Do not allow the family of Pelops to be blotted out.
Save us—and then, in spite of death, you are not dead;
for children are a man's living name and fame, though

> he be gone; they are like the corks that buoy up a fish-
> erman's net, saving his knotted lines from sinking deep.
> ELECTRA: Listen! It is in your behalf that we cry out. Answer
> our prayer and you save yourself.
>
> (ll. 500–509)

Agamemnon in his grave has the most urgent of reasons to be concerned for the success of Orestes' enterprise: his life depends on it. The
*oikos* must be rescued from a corporate extinction which will sweep away
living and dead together. Therefore the price of failure is death—a sinking
into cold, hungry oblivion for Agamemnon, and for Orestes the annihilation of the childless exile who "dies" absolutely, outside his family:

> Unhonoured of all men, friendless, he perishes at last shrivelled
> pitifully by a death that wastes him utterly away.
>
> (ll. 295–96)

If Orestes fails to recover the headship of the house of Atreus he will be,
as he says elsewhere, "an alien utterly, for ever," cut off from the collective
life apart from which the idea of personal destiny is meaningless: his
image of the lopped-off member slowly withering to nothing is well
chosen. He looks to the family and the family looks to him, for he is its
"hope of a seed that shall not perish, longed for with tears"; together
they live, and apart they die. This one great death threatening all brings
us to acknowledge the foundations of social solidarity on which the *Oresteia* is built. It has nothing in common with single deaths which are
events within the life of the group, lived through by the group, and of
interest for Greek tragedy only exceptionally, because of the forms they
take. Death is prominent in the *Antigone* of Sophocles because burial has
been refused to Polyneices' body; in his *Oedipus at Colonus* because the
processes of death have been altered for the sanctified old king, and a
mystery surrounds his leaving life on earth; in the *Agamemnon* because
the head of a great house, king and military commander, has been butchered by a woman with an axe, and then mourning rites have been with-
held from him. Shorn of special public circumstances, the death of a man
does not hold great power over Greek intelligence and imagination; and
this is not surprising since death does not present them with the fearful
alternative of personal immortality and personal annihilation. It is the
perfect solitude brought upon each of us by the thought of dying that
makes death the tragic fact we know.

But Orestes, in the great scene in which he kills Aegisthus offstage and then enters to confront his mother, carries a collective destiny which it is the function of the ever-present Chorus to hold before us throughout. Their fear recalls the earlier image of a ship in danger of foundering, and their resentment the later one of a horse held in by its rider's "great curb-chain." When at last a man's cry sounds from inside the palace, they ask: "How goes it? How has the issue been determined for the house?" (which makes hideous English; but such translations as Professor George Thomson's "How does it go within?" weaken the corporate focus un-acceptably)—and Orestes emerges victorious to face Clytemnestra. She urges the mother-son relation upon him:

> CLYTEMNESTRA: Your life I cherished, and with you I wish to
>     live out my own.
> ORESTES: What! Kill my father and then share my house?
>
> (ll. 908–9)

His retort exposes the *oikos*-rooted impossibility of sparing her life. She and Aegisthus are a "polluted pair," and the killing of them is a kind of surgical operation in which the diseased part of the household's body is cut away. With Aegisthus there is no more to it than that: he has "suffered the adulterer's punishment as the law allows." But Clytemnestra's case is different. She is Orestes' mother and he cannot kill her without bringing upon himself a singularly heinous form of blood-guilt: "my victory," as he neatly puts it, "is a pollution."

We see a pattern established early in the *Agamemnon* reappearing at the end of the second play of the trilogy. Agamemnon had either to sacrifice his daughter or abandon the Trojan expedition—both courses involving him in guilt. Orestes, in the next generation, has to kill his mother, but he cannot do this without making himself answerable to the Furies, the pre-Olympian chthonic goddesses whose chief office is to punish those who have shed kindred blood. This second dilemma of the trilogy falls inside the action, unlike the first, and is more fully articulated. Orestes' compulsion to matricide is urged throughout at the level of the house's present desperate sickness; he comes as the healer from within. And to this necessity Aeschylus adds a second, of duty towards Agamemnon performed in obedience to divine command; Apollo has charged Orestes to kill his father's murderers, warning him that he will be pursued by the Furies who have been roused by this earlier killing within the family, if he fails in his duty: so that he must offend his mother's Furies by acting and his father's Furies by doing nothing. We find, as in the *Agamemnon,* a parallel working of human and superhuman logics, and Aeschylus shows wonderful art in his disclosure of the full religio-social complex during the few lines of dialogue which culminate in Orestes forcing Clytemnestra into the palace for the vengeance-killing. Orestes has a companion in the *Libation-Bearers,* a young man of about his own age called Pylades. Pylades is quite unlike any stage-figure in Greek tragedy. He enters with Orestes and remains onstage almost continuously; but he says nothing. The silence of Orestes' friend is something we grow used to; it has become a settled feature of the dramatic scene long before Orestes confronts his mother; and now, four-fifths of the way through the play, Clytemnestra and Orestes are talking and Pylades is standing by, and Orestes turns to Pylades and asks: "What shall I do, Pylades? Shall reverence for motherhood hold me back? Shall I spare her?" and Pylades speaks for the first and only time:

> Then what will become of Apollo's Pythian oracles? And of our covenants pledged on oath? Count all men your enemies rather than the gods.
>
> (ll. 899–902)

Our shock at this unexpected finding of voice is a pale reflection of what a fifth-century audience must have felt. Their theatre worked with three actors, and a sharp distinction was inevitable, in dramaturgy and in play-watching, between speaking parts (taken by the actors, with necessary doublings) and mutes. Some of the mutes of Greek tragedy are impressive presences—but they are mute. Conversely, some of the speaking parts are very slight, but there are no half measures over their speaking: you do not find characters with only two or three lines to utter. Pylades is the only exception to this rule; he begins and continues like a mute, and nobody watching the *Libation-Bearers* from within the Greek convention, as Pylades is introduced and repeatedly indicated without responding, can doubt that he is a mute; so that Aeschylus has secured the most complete arrest of attention, a stopping of dramatic time, for Orestes' direct, inescapable question: "What shall I do, Pylades?"

Commentators, finding a touch of nature here, explain that Orestes has been moved by his mother's appeal, face to face, and is faltering in his resolve to kill her; and they remain strangely uninterested in the unique pseudo-mute who is being thrust into speech. "What shall I do?" flows not from inner uncertainty but from the need to achieve full exposure of the Oresteian dilemma; we should conceive the thing from the standpoint of dramaturgic policy, situationally. The dialogue between mother and son sustains the *oikos*-theme in the generalising way of Aeschylean stichomythia:

> CLYTEMNESTRA: But you must not mention my sins without mentioning your father's too.
> ORESTES: But you must not accuse one who laboured while you were sitting idle at home.
> CLYTEMNESTRA: It is a hard thing, my child, for women to be deprived of a husband.
> ORESTES: Yet it is the man's effort which supports them while they stay at home.
>
> (ll. 918–21)

and states the simple and, at this stage, ultimate opposition of mother's Furies to father's:

> CLYTEMNESTRA: Watch out! Beware the hounds that avenge a mother.
> ORESTES: And the hounds that avenge a father—how shall I escape them if I leave this deed undone?
>
> (ll. 924–25)

But Apollo's command—the Olympian echo, as it were, of the human and chthonian debates—does not arise between them. That is left to Pylades; and in his one utterance we sense an awful authority, as if the god had possessed the seeming-mute and spoken through him.

Questions like this "What shall I do?," building up the dramatic moment *ab extra,* are common in Aeschylus. Earlier in the *Libation-Bearers,* the Chorus are telling Orestes that Clytemnestra has had an ill-omened dream:

> ORESTES: Have you heard what the dream was? Can you tell it right?
> CHORUS: She dreamt she gave birth to a snake—that is her own account.
> ORESTES: What followed? How does the story end?
> CHORUS: She swaddled it and laid it to rest like a little child.
> ORESTES: What food did it crave, the new-born venomous brute?
> CHORUS: In her dream she offered it her breast.
> ORESTES: Surely her nipple was wounded by the loathsome thing?

CHORUS: Yes; with the milk it drew forth clots of blood.

(ll. 526–33)

Orestes is very plainly prompting, he is not asking, and the function of a line like "What food did it crave . . . ," cast in question form, is to coax into the open an aspect of Clytemnestra's dream which the dramatist wants mentioned. This kind of exchange is first cousin to epic narrative in that the information that emerges serves the unfolding tale and not the questioner's ignorance. Which is not, of course, to argue that the questioner knows the answer, that Orestes turns to Pylades with his mind irrevocably made up: rather, that the modern critical sensibility grasping at a Hamletish indecision finds itself empty-handed. We have to direct outward and institutionalise the horror and disgust and contempt of Shakespeare's "Almost as bad, good mother, As kill a king and marry with his brother" in order to understand where Aeschylus is laying his finger in "What! Kill my father and then share my house?"; and similarly, when Orestes asks "What shall I do, Pylades?," we can only follow the question into the contemplated and imminent deed, a further facet of which Pylades is about to illuminate and where poetry and meaning reside. It will be objected that "contemplated" admits the play of consciousness upon possibilities of action, and in a way this is just. But the consciousness here admitted refers us to the watchman's thought at the beginning of the trilogy; "And yet the house itself, could it but speak, would have a plain tale to tell"; the voices of humanity are the fragmented voice of the house of Atreus, and for the outraged and judging *oikos* the vengeance-killing of Clytemnestra is both a necessity and another terrible self-wounding. If we think of Orestes contemplating his deed, we must also remember that he is "the eye of the house." The Chorus's vision of him coming as the healer from within was, they now see, premature. Not proved false, of course, but judgment waits on the event as he defiles his hands with kindred blood, doing what must be done. The image of a storm beating against the house reappears. Orestes rushes out, pursued by the Furies. He goes to seek ritual cleansing from Apollo, and the Chorus are left wondering, in the closing lines of the *Libation-Bearers,* whether Orestes is in truth "a deliverer—or shall I say a doom?" (ll. 1073–74).

This question is answered in the *Eumenides* where Orestes is formally brought to trial by the Furies and acquitted by a court of law constituted for this occasion. Apollo, divine counsel for the defence, urges an honest count of votes with the solemn insistence: "the cast of a single vote has been known to raise a fallen house." Thus the issue proves happy in which the single and the corporate fates are united, and Orestes' self-pollution through killing his mother is not finally ruinous. Aeschylus binds his third play to his second by means of Orestes' pollution, presenting a full life-cycle, from its inception at Clytemnestra's killing—the criminal duty, the "victory" which is also "a pollution"—to its departure confirmed (or perhaps effected) by the trial verdict. The staging of its initial attachment to Orestes deserves close attention. He follows his mother's death with a statement of his doubts and fears to the Chorus. They reply, firmly: "No, you have done well . . ." (*Libation-Bearers,* l. 1044); and at once he gives a shout of terror, for he has seen the Furies. Then this dialogue takes place:

> CHORUS: What fancies are troubling you, best of sons to Aga-
> memnon? Bear up; you must not let fear completely get
> the better of you.
> ORESTES: No fancies, these troubles—not to me. The hounds
> that avenge mother-slaying are here, plain for me to see.
> CHORUS: The blood on your hands is still fresh: that explains
> your deranged mind.
> ORESTES: More and more—O lord Apollo—swarms of them.
> Look! And their eyes weep bloody pus.
> CHORUS: You have one way of being cleansed: Apollo's touch
> will rid you of this affliction.
> ORESTES: You do not see them—but I do. They are after me;
> I must escape.
>
> (ll. 1051–62)

Orestes sees the Furies because his mother's blood is fresh on his hands, and when he has been cleansed by Apollo he will cease to see them. The Furies are subjective manifestations in the sense that they appear only to Orestes, but they have objective status in that their visible presence is grounded in the material human blood on his hands: they cannot be called figments of his imagination any more than the blood can be so called. It is most important to respect the relation between blood and Furies established in this dialogue because we are thus warned to eschew the subject/object dichotomy whereby we normally interpret such appearances (old Hamlet's ghost is objective, Banquo's is subjective) and which is prevalent in modern Aeschylean criticism. To summarise, commentators conceive the Furies to exist at some point on a line extending from pure subjective fantasy to pure objective fact; they disagree as to the location of this point (those who believe in a primitive Aeschylus place it near the objective extreme, those who see him attaining or groping towards the idea of the troubled conscience place it towards the other end), but they do not doubt that the image of the subject-object line is a satisfactory one for the conduct of their argument. Nevertheless, the coupling of blood and Furies indicates that this image provides a false frame of reference, or, if it is to be retained, that the objective correlate of Orestes' solitary vision compels us to place the Furies at both ends of the line simultaneously; for the solitude of his vision is not the solitude of an unshared hallucination, but the solitude of this one pair of bloody hands.

In fact we may avoid all these complexities by allowing Orestes' physical defilement and his seeing of the Furies to make their impact together, in a naively immediate way, as they do at the end of the *Libation-Bearers*. Seeing the Furies is proof of a kind of guilt, and having bloody hands evidences defilement; the culpable state of being is continuous with its manifestations, and Aeschylus and his society provide us with a single term embracing both: pollution. Moreover, the logic of pollution, the defilement-guilt unity, applies to the Furies as well as to Orestes; they pursue him (that is, they react to the mother-slaying) because of the physical taint, being represented in the *Eumenides* as tracking him down by the scent of blood upon him.

The reader of the *Oresteia* is under pressure—from himself as well as from the critical tradition—to convert pollution into something more familiar; it comes easier to make the Chorus tell Orestes that the shock and horror of the killing have produced an hallucination—the vision is "mental," the Furies aren't really there—than to follow Aeschylus in a simple going-together of defiled hands and apparition-assaulted consciousness. The more comfortable idea matches a double standard of inward guilt and outward defilement, the less comfortable and the correct, a single standard of pollution; and the need to discriminate between the more and the less comfortable idea is proved by the false double standard leading to a wilderness of subject/object dissensions and to a near-systematic rewriting of the *Eumenides*. The rending in two of Aeschylean pollution has focussed attention on a contradiction which the most casual reader cannot fail to notice. At the end of the *Libation-Bearers* Orestes rushes out, bloody-handed and pursued by the Furies, to present himself at the shrine of Apollo for ritual cleansing. The opening of the *Eumenides* finds him at the shrine where the god receives him as a suppliant for purification and where the ceremony duly takes place. In consequence of this Orestes maintains firmly throughout the play that he is no longer polluted. Apollo supports him in this argument, and Athena, the goddess-judge of the case, expressly recognises that the rites have been effective (ll. 473–75). All would be clear and consistent did not Aeschylus give us an Orestes who is still, in dramatic fact, polluted—still dripping blood, still drawing the Furies after him by its smell, still (in the Furies' words) with a dark cloud of pollution hanging over him which makes it impossible for him to return to his house or take part in common worship.

This is the collision of facts—of effective cleansing with continuing pollution—which has exercised commentators. Some of Verrall's furthest flights were inspired by his unwillingness to believe that so mature a thinker as Aeschylus would have Orestes dripping with his mother's blood months after he has killed her. Verrall explained the blood at one point—there is no denying that it is there in the text—as that of animals Orestes has sacrificed, and at another as Orestes' own; the wandering exile has cut his feet on the long walk from Apollo's shrine at Delphi to Athens, or his exhaustion has brought on an internal haemorrhage and he is bleeding at the mouth. These theories would not resolve the contradiction even if they were acceptable (since they fail to explain why Orestes is still polluted), but they do reveal the false double standard at work. They buy a sophisticated interpretation of Orestes' guilt or innocence at the cost of a primitive interpretation of the Furies and the defiling blood; the guilty state is severed from the bloodstained hands, leaving the commentator free to spiritualise the former and banish the latter to a world of crude material superstitions in which blood—any blood—attracts the Furies who are to be found following each and every trail with the abandon of ill-trained hounds. We end by supposing that Aeschylus and other enlightened spirits understood the *Oresteia* at the level of guilt and innocence, and the fifth-century groundlings at the level of defilement and purgation.

The sophisticated and the primitive worlds are both fictions erected on the grave of Aeschylean pollution; they bear no relation to his text, and so the text is manipulated into rough and ready conformity to the fictions. We are told that "'purgation' is a survival and has little reality" in Aeschylus's story because the commentator has trapped himself into maintaining that purgation has nothing more serious than defilement, nothing more pregnant with mind, to which it can minister. And although the contradiction between Orestes' ritual purgation and his continuing pollution is not resolved in this way, it is rendered tolerable by

being assigned to that part of the story or to a level of treatment which
Aeschylus did not greatly care about. Thus the issue is cheapened by a
procedure which is as slovenly as it is dishonest. Paradoxically, it is by
giving the contradiction its full value that its dramatic function becomes
intelligible. What must remain an absurdity on the plane of defilement
(how can Orestes be both clean and unclean?) grows into a sudden imaginative harmony on that of psycho-physical pollution where the relation
of unclean hands and soul is one of continuity, and not of primitive and
sophisticated levels of dramaturgy or of symbolic parallelism or of anything else. Indeed, the famous contradiction is our assurance that Aeschylus accepts and respects this simple continuity, that he lives within it
and imagines through it; for the terrible doubleness of Orestes' position
is faithfully rendered in the actuality of his cleansed and still-polluted
hands.

With Orestes as with Agamemnon, Aeschylus returns the answer
yes and no to our question "Is he guilty?"; and again we have to purge
the question of all individualistic preconceiving in order to read the answer right. This means, primarily, a resolute containment of revenge
when we regard Orestes' act, and, when we study its consequences, an
ability to see him with the household's eyes—to stand with the domestic
slave-women of the Chorus, waiting to see whether he will prove a deliverer or a doom—before we call the tragedy his. It is a mistake to
suppose that the Furies' persecution of him is inspired by personal ma-
lignity, very much as it is a mistake to give a Hamletish twist to "What!
Kill my father and then share my house?" Their statement at the trial,
in answer to Apollo's defence of Orestes, has the same foundation of
social and institutional impossibility as his retort to his mother:

> Just consider the meaning of your plea for his acquittal. Shall
> one who has spilt blood of kin, his mother's blood, on the
> ground—shall he afterwards live in his father's house in Ar-
> gos? Shall he take part in public worship, at altars and where
> kinsfolk wash in holy water?
>
> (ll. 652–56)

The house cannot keep the mother or recover the son: this is the centre
of distress and the full significance of the threat to the life, or life-in-
death, of the wandering exile. The *montage* of the choral lyric is not
random:

> Dark is the cloud of pollution hovering over the man, and rumour carried on voices of mourning proclaims that a mist-thick gloom covers his house.
>
> (ll. 377–80)

The false critical refinement that spiritualises psycho-physical pollution into a more tractable notion of guilt attenuates the dramatic object miserably, and recalls the fate of the carpet scene in the *Agamemnon*. We may venture the general observation that the boundaries of the self in Greek and especially Aeschylean tragedy are more fluid than we allow. In the *Libation-Bearers,* when Electra discovers a lock of hair which Orestes has cut off as a religious offering, when she holds it up and notes its likeness to her own hair and dares to wonder if it might be her brother's, the scene somehow confounds our sense of the pathetic; and insight into this strangeness comes later in the play when Orestes produces the robe in which Agamemnon was murdered, has it spread out, indicts Clytemnestra by it, ponders what name to call it ("a trap for a wild beast . . . a corpse's shroud . . . a hunting-net") and brings it into the foreground of his lament for his father, by which he sets right the denial of observances at his death: "Now at last I am here to speak his praises, to make lament for my father as I address the robe that brought death to him" (ll. 980–1015). The Penguin translator does right to bring out the stand-in function of the robe—as the translator with a critical axe to grind does not feel entitled to attempt:

> I offer now my lament, since I may not see his body,
> To this treacherous web that caught and killed my father.

For he thus exposes the source of the incident's mysterious power (to which many who have seen the trilogy will testify) in the robe's effective communion with the long-dead king its wearer. The scene is a beckoning forward of the murdered man, to which we respond through our vestigial awareness of the communion under discussion—an awareness evidenced by the fascination of the personal possessions of the dead or absent, and even by that obscure sense of a falling away from self, mixed with a lingering self-identity, which a man experiences at the sight of his hair on the floor of a barber's shop. Aeschylus affects us in this hidden way, through an exploitation of the nebulous fringe of selfhood which is very much more eloquent than anything we are able to summon from within ourselves: confident in its articulation, not in any sense fugitive or irrational. We leave our world of subjective pathos—of Constance's "Grief fills the room up of my absent child. . . . Stuffs out his vacant garments with his form"—for a new, and immeasurably old, literalism (*King John*, 3.4.93).

We respond more readily to Orestes' lock of hair and Agamemnon's robe, where the communion of self with object is individual, than we do to the purple carpet of the *Agamemnon* whose capacity to suffer outrage is commensurate with its *oikos*-determined dignity. A carpet is a carpet until it is shown to be something more—and the something more being in this case the body, the psycho-physical substance, of the house of Atreus, we do not experience the same degree of subliminal receptiveness. The consequent undervaluing of Clytemnestra's economic hubris and the self-wounding of the house in the *Agamemnon* is matched by the personalistic, revenge-dominated view of Orestes' exploit in the *Libation-Bearers*. Against this we have urged the corporate fight for health and life, and the single great death threatening all. But the persistence of the economic strand ought also to be noted. Orestes' account of himself "turned brute-savage by the forfeiture of my inheritance" (l. 275) has embarrassed commentators and led to fanciful glossing of its plain sense because it looks unworthy, selfish, greedy, to the eye that can only follow the material and spiritual strands in separation. For Orestes, there is nothing incongruous in coupling the incentives of "the god's command and my great grief for my father and with these the pinch of poverty" (ll. 300–301); nor for Electra in expressing the pity of her brother's plight through his "being held from his patrimony" (ll. 135–36). The *oikos*-theme is one.

And a certain consistency appears also in the present discussion. For the robe and lock of hair and carpet and whole family wealth, saturated in individual or corporate selfhood, acquire their value through the same apprehension of outward and inward continuity that produces the moral logic of pollution. The thrusting outward of the self into a world of "mere" objects reciprocates the power of blood on the hands to taint the soul. Indeed the earlier warning against imposing a subject-object dichotomy on Aeschylus ought to be framed more widely, until his entire dramatic universe is placed in a middleground of the imagination where not only are objects *psyche*-drenched but human subjects objectify, externalise themselves—at first sight very strangely. Electra greets Orestes, when he has revealed himself to her after years of separation and misery, with a declaration of love. This takes the form of a statement that she has "four shares" or parts of love to bestow on him—the share her father would have had were he alive, the share her mother has forfeited, the share that would have gone to her sister Iphigeneia, and his own share as her brother. It is as if her love, or herself loving, were made up into four undelivered parcels which Orestes now appropriates. This picture of the individual's emotional life (which would not have surprised Aristotle) strikes quaint and cold to us who are strangers, almost, to the multiple self, and who take an inward concentration (our Electra would nurse a single flame of love deep within her) for selfhood's principle. Nor have we the containing *oikos* to vivify Electra's dry scheme of family relations, and to counterbalance the faint personal self with the strength of the collective consciousness. The house is a horse reined in by a cruel rider; it is a ship weltering in heavy seas; it is a building in a storm; it is a human being lifting up her eyes in joy to welcome the deliverer. Aeschylus gives to Clytemnestra (silencing consideration of her sincerity as he does so) the image, only very gently roused and then as gently parted from, of a tree whose life has shrunk back into its root in Agamemnon's absence, now nourished and brought to its full being by his return:

> The root still lives, and the leaves return to spread over the house a shade against the dog-star: such is your homecoming to your house's hearth—a sign of warmth in winter. Yes, and when Zeus is making wine from the bitter grape, then at once there is coolness in the house when its undoubted lord moves about his halls.
>
> (*Agamemnon*, ll. 966–72)

A fitting commentary on the *oikos*-theme, and on the poetic dramatist's power to render the house clear through (not in spite of) an extreme conceptual imprecision—a unity of elements whose cooperative diversity is its life.

# The Commos in the *Libation-Bearers*

## Anne Lebeck

These are the problems of the commos: its relation to the preceding scene between Orestes, Electra, and the chorus is not spelled out. Before the lament begins, Orestes has declared a willingness to obey the oracle and avenge his father. Therefore the commos might seem to have no place for doubt or resolution. And if this is the case, the lyric would appear to lack in purpose, lose in point; content and sense be crushed beneath its length, its complexity of form and obscurity of language. The following analysis attempts to determine the connection between trimeter and lyric, then to ascertain the latter's function, a reason for the importance of its place within the drama. Put briefly, the commos explores two aspects of the coming action: vengeance is matricide, vengeance is just.

### DILEMMA AND DECISION

The last lines which Orestes speaks before the commos (ll. 297–305) stand in close relation to the lyric. His speech opens with an assurance to the chorus that Apollo's oracle, which commands that he pass through this peril, will not betray him (ll. 269–70). There follows an account of the punishment foretold by that same oracle should he neglect to slay the slayers of his father. The speech closes with question, answer, and the reasons for that answer: a deliberation on the necessity of vengeance.

---

From The Oresteia: *A Study in Language and Structure.* © 1971 by the Trustees of Harvard University. Harvard University Press, 1971.

τοιοῖσδε χρησμοῖς ἆρα χρὴ πεποιθέναι;
κεἰ μὴ πέποιθα, τοὔργον ἔστ' ἐργαστέον.
(ll. 297–298)

The question: "Am I bound to put my trust in the oracles which bind
me to this course?" The answer: "Even if I trust them not, the deed
must still be done."

The question involves more than the credibility of those penalties
described in lines 271–96. It refers to the oracle as a whole, to the injunction that vengeance be taken no less than the punishment prophesied
for disobedience. Thus Orestes begins with a confident assertion that
Apollo's oracle will not betray him to his enemies, will not play him
false; at the end he asks whether that oracle can be trusted. In the re-
mainder of the speech he explains his answer to this question, disposing
of the doubt that lies behind it.

Even should the oracle prove unreliable or false, the task must still
be undertaken. The command and threat of Apollo are not his sole support; there are personal motives whose power is no less irresistible. "For
many desires lead here to one conclusion: the god's command and mourning for my father, deeply felt, and there is too the pinch of want—that
my countrymen, everywhere renowned, much honored as the ravagers
of Troy, no longer serve two women" (ll. 299–304). In these words freedom and necessity, divine will and human wish, are interwoven. Orestes
raises personal feeling to the level of impersonal necessity. He does not
say, "Oracle or no oracle I myself desire to act" but "Oracle or no oracle
this act *must* be performed because of the following desires." At the same
time, a god's command rests on a par with human longing: πολλοὶ γὰρ
... ἵμεροι, / θεοῦ τ' ἐφετμαὶ [various . . . desires and the commands of
the God] (ll. 299–300). There is a point at which constraint and choice
converge; in man's own will the gods find Fate's accomplice.

The reasons with which Orestes justifies his answer form the subject
matter of the commos. The ἵμεροι [desires] compelling him to avenge
Agamemnon's murder reappear as motifs prescribed by the ritual of
funeral lament and invocation hymn. The commos itself is the "grief for
my father" (l. 300); "pressing want" (l. 301) becomes the plaint of strai-
tened circumstances and dispossession (ll.336–37, 407–8, 444–45). Lines
302–4, the desire that the glorious (εὐκλεεστάτους) conquerors of Troy
should not be humbled, echo in a motif which links the first two strophes
of Orestes: the funeral dirge in celebration of past glory, γόος εὐκλεὴς /
†προσθοδόμοις Ἀτρείδαις (ll. 321–22), and the wish that Agamemnon

had perished beneath the walls of Troy and thus left glory, εὔκλεια, to his house (ll. 345–48).

In the commos those feelings which force Orestes to his decision are made present, the whole process of decision acted out. As uncertainty (ll. 315–39) and wishful thinking (ll. 345–71) are overcome, the prayer for vengeance grows more explicit until, toward the close of the lyric, the resolution to take vengeance is reached again.

One might argue, as Reinhardt has, that because Orestes has already expressed his willingness to act before the commos, the commos itself cannot deal with conflict and decision. Such a view fails to take account of the relationship between trimeter and lyric, the timeless quality of the latter. This relation cannot be expressed by the words before and after. The commos exists on a different level from the dialogue, exploring in depth what is already stated, the question asked and answered in lines 297–304. And even when a decision has been made, relapse remains a possibility, a possibility realized in line 899.

According to Schadewaldt, except for that one moment's hesitation (l. 899), the decision of Orestes stays constant throughout. The play's development lies not in a decision reached after inner struggle but in an unwavering resolve which grows clearer and more believable with the addition of each new detail. "Nicht der Mensch ist zu Anfang weniger entschlossen, dann mehr und völlig, sondern das Bild seiner Entschlossenheit ist zuerst gleichsam nur im umriss da, dann öffnet es seine Gründe, gewinnt bestimmtere, tiefere, leidenschaftlichere Züge." Thus stated his interpretation may seem to differ little from that presented here; the difference is one of emphasis. (This applies only to his ultimate conclusions; as far as individual passages are concerned, we are in complete disaccord.) The decision of Orestes is not static and unchanging. It grows in depth, takes on new dimension, as he faces the fact of matricide and explores the dilemma of right action which is wrong. Each new statement is stronger than the preceding because made on the basis of greater insight, less equivocation.

Explaining why "this deed must be done" there is one reason which Orestes does not give: the law of Dike, δράσαντι παθεῖν, [like for like], demands it. In the commos, from their opening anapests, the Chorus instruct him in this law, urging that it is just to follow the dictates of Apollo and his own desire. In line 899 the same task of stilling doubt falls to Pylades; he confirms Orestes' original resolve with a reminder of the divine injunction and its prior claim to man's affection. This is the part played by the Chorus during the commos. They reveal the universal code which lies behind Apollo's oracle; under their tutelage Orestes gains greater understanding of the constraint imposed upon him and reaffirms his readiness to act: "She'll pay for dishonoring my father, with the gods' willing aid, with will and aid of my own hands. And having slain her, may *I* perish" (ll. 435–38). He can accept his task for what it is, the murder of his mother, because the Chorus have convinced him that this task is just.

Thus through the commos Orestes gains insight into the paradox of Dike and his own dilemma. Led by the exhortations of the Chorus he experiences the intense emotion accompanying such insight, the πάθος which culminates in μάθος [The suffering (páthos) which culminates in learning (máthos).] And at the end he restates his decision in terms of Dike: Ἄρης Ἄρει ξυμβαλεῖ, Δίκα Δίκα. Right will clash with Right (l. 461). An Orestes free from doubt and hesitation, unaware that he is trapped by conflicting claims, sure that right is entirely on his side— such an Orestes is not the hero of the *Oresteia,* a trilogy which turns upon the necessity of disastrous choice. However, it would perhaps be well to stress once more that "Orestes' dilemma" is not presented as moral revulsion from Apollo's command. Rather it is the problem posed by an act simultaneously right and wrong.

The commos, then, is a lyrical statement of the forces which lead to decision, a study of dilemma and choice. The decision expressed in lines 435–38 and line 461 is at once the same and different from that which introduced the commos: Orestes repeats his resolve with full awareness of its right and wrong. Man has this freedom within the limits of necessity; it is a freedom attained through understanding, an understanding gained at the price of suffering.

## Matricide: The Problem Faced

As invocation hymn the commos has a double purpose: to awaken the wrath of the dead king and, simultaneously, that of his living avenger. The two are really one: the μῆνις [the wrath (mēnis)] of Agamemnon becomes incarnate in his son, its human agent. The dead man's spirit, now powerless and dark, must be roused to anger, urged to action. Orestes too is powerless, faced by a problem without solution, called upon to perform an act at once just and unjust. The same forces of vengeance must be conjured up from the depths of his own soul, strengthening the decision already reached, transforming thought into execution.

Orestes' doubt and hesitancy, his aversion from the act of matricide, are manifest at line 899 when he turns from Clytemnestra with the words, "What can I do? Shall I not shrink from murder of my mother?" In the first section of the commos these feelings find oblique expression in the form of a ritual lament. Orestes' uncertainty about reaching the dead with words (ll. 315–22), his despair about the present and vain desire to alter the past (ll. 345–53), the hopelessness of his appeal to Zeus (ll. 408–9), the wish to perish (l. 438): these are conventional motifs. They are here used to suggest the individual's inner conflict; the commos is a cry of despair at once ritual and personal.

The very structure of the lyric reflects movement toward renewed resolve, suggests doubt overcome. The first section (ll. 315–422) is triadic and epirrhematic. In each of the four triads a choral strophe of encouragement is surrounded by the despairing strophe and antistrophe of Orestes and Electra. The effect is that of a vicious circle. The triads are punctuated by three anapestic epirrhemata, probably delivered by the coryphaeus, which add further exhortation. Thus the form is ABA-epirrhema-CBC-epirrhema-DED-epirrhema-FEF. The first triad (ABA) is closely connected with the second (CBC) both formally (by responsion of B, the choral strophe) and by similarity of content. The same close relation obtains between the third and fourth triads, which mark increase of confidence on the part of Orestes. The second epirrhema (ll. 372–79) serves as a dividing line between the first two triads and the second two. Its importance in changing the attitude of Orestes and Electra is underlined by length (eight as opposed to the five lines of its fellows) and a more complex metrical pattern.

In the second section (ll. 423–55) Electra, herself convinced, joins forces with the chorus. One after another they urge Orestes. The preceding triadic form gives way to a strophic pair of three stanzas each, the strophes of brother and sister no longer in responsion. Form: A (Chorus) B (Electra) C (Orestes) // C (Chorus) A (Electra) B (Chorus). Here Orestes regains his purpose, repeats his decision with new intensity.

In the third and last section (ll. 456–79) Orestes, Electra, and the Chorus form a single will, united by the desire for vengeance: στάσις δὲ πάγκοινος ἅδ᾽ ἐπιρροθεῖ [Gathered together in revolt we shout our approval]. The first strophic pair consists of a line delivered by Orestes, one by Electra, and three by the Chorus. The last strophe and antistrophe are sung by the Chorus alone. The despair which they now voice at the curse upon Agamemnon's house (ll. 466–75) echoes the earlier despair of Orestes at his own dilemma, the climax of that curse. An actual attempt to conjure up the ghost does not begin until after the commos

and is performed by Orestes and Electra alone. The Chorus retire to the
background, their task accomplished.

Another line of development, running parallel with that discussed
above, can be traced through the commos to the critical moment which
puts Orestes' purpose to a test. During the lyric the justice of vengeance
is set forth; at the same time this just vengeance reveals itself as matricide,
a greater crime than that which it must punish. The figure of Clytemnestra is slowly detached from Aegisthus until at last she stands alone,
true object of the coming retribution. The full implication of the act is
brought out first by avoidance, finally by use, of the word μάτηρ [mother
(máter)].

In the earlier decision Orestes does not refer to Clytemnestra as his
mother or speak of her alone. He calls the murderers "two women"
(l. 304). Such plurals are used consistently throughout the early scenes
and at the beginning of the commos: τοῖς αἰτίοις (l. 117), τοὺς κταν-
όντας (l. 144), τοὺς αἰτίους (l. 273), οἱ κτανόντες (l. 367), τῶν ... κρατούντων (l. 377). The relationship of child and parent then rises slowly
to the surface. Only by virtue of this relation is the act of vengeance a
tragic act. If the murder were not matricide, there would be no conflict
between right and right, a choice impossible for man to make.

Allusion to parentage is at first obscure. Both Electra and Orestes
avoid the word "mother," using shadowy substitutes instead: τοκεῖς,
τεκόμενοι [Parents (tokeîs), "Those who brought us into the world"
(tekómenoi)], plural and indefinite. These words are made more prominent by the ambiguity which attends their use.

## FULFILLMENT FOR THE PARENT

In the third and fourth triads (ll. 380–422), wish to alter the past
gives way to wish for future retribution. Orestes' first strophe here is a
response to the hortatory anapests of the Chorus which precede it. Their
words like arrows penetrate his ear, stinging him to prayer for vengeance:

> τοῦτο διαμπερὲς οὖς
> ἵκεθ' ἅπερ τε βέλος.
> Ζεῦ Ζεῦ, κάτωθεν ἀμπέμπων
> ὑστερόποινον ἄταν.

[This cry has come to your ear
like a deep driven arrow.
Zeus, Zeus, force up from below
ground the delayed destruction.]
(ll. 380–83)

In lines 286–90 he spoke of that dark arrow (βέλος) with which the Furies strike and derange the man who leaves kin murder unavenged. The words of the Chorus have just such an effect upon him and the last lines of his own strophe are difficult to interpret; lines with multiple meaning usually do present such difficulty.

Both the strophe of Orestes and the preceding line of the Chorus are ominous in undertone. The Chorus end the commos filled with dread, mourning the outcome of that act which they long advocated (ll. 466–70). The sense of doom with which the commos closes, foreknowledge fulfilled at the end of the play, has its place as well in passages like these. By virtue of their ambiguity they touch upon the problem of Dike, the dilemma of Orestes, the inevitable disaster.

Contrast and parallelism suggest a connection between line 379 of the chorus and line 385 of Orestes:

παισὶ δὲ μᾶλλον γεγένηται
τοκεῦσι δ' ὅμως τελεῖται.

[Paisí dè mâllon gegénētai
Tokeûsi d' homōs teleîtai]

Rose makes a revelatory comment about 379. He remarks that μᾶλλον [mâllon] is without reference and, to illustrate his point, translates, "For Agamemnon's children it is more—what?" The obscurity of the line serves a purpose: to raise this question. With μᾶλλον [mâllon] Rose and Groeneboom understand στυγερόν [Stugerón (loathsome, abominable)] from the preceding line:

τῶν μὲν ἀρωγοὶ
κατὰ γῆς ἤδη, τῶν δὲ κρατούντων
χέρες οὐχ ὅσιαι †στυγερῶν τούτων.

[Powers gather under ground
to give aid. The hands of those who are lords
are unclean, and these are loathsome (stugerón)]
(ll. 376–78)

The situation is more hateful to the children (than it was for Agamemnon, Rose; that it is for the Chorus, Groeneboom). Verrall takes the line to mean, "'the thing is done' or 'the effect is produced for children more (than it could be for those who are not).' γεγένηται [gegénētai], *it is effected,* represents, according to the habit of the language, merely something (to be determined by the context) which could be expressed by a passive verb, here therefore that 'the aid of the subterranean spirits is secured.'" The Chorus may have intended either of these meanings but because they do not fully express their thought, the line suggests a significance other than the one intended. γίγνεται [gegnētai], used impersonally, means "it befalls, comes about, happens." "Impure are the hands of the mighty, the hated; and it has befallen the children still more." A crime more impious, a greater sacrilege, has fallen to the lot of Agamemnon's children than that of which his murderers are guilty.

Scholarly opinion on the meaning of line 385 is sharply divided. Should τοκεῦσι [Tokeûsi] be taken as a "true plural, in a general statement; whatever is meant by the whole phrase is true for parents as for others, or is true for the guilty, parents though they may be"? If, instead, the plural is used for singular, does it refer to the mother or the father? Or could there be a reference to punishment as child of crime, the offspring resembling its parent?

In their efforts to determine the exact meaning, commentators have overlooked one point: what is the function of a line that lends itself so well to antithetical interpretations (father/mother)? Although τοκεύς [Tokeús] means "father" in the singular, the plural means not "fathers" but "parents," father and mother together. τοκεῦσι δ' ὅμως τελεῖται [Tokeûsi d' homōs teleîtai] applies to both parents: fulfillment of revenge for the father, for the mother penalty paid in full. And this is the dilemma of Orestes. The task of avenging his father entails wronging his mother; he cannot do one without the other.

The entire strophe which this line concludes has ominous implications:

> τοῦτο διαμπερὲς οὖς
> ἵκεθ' ἅπερ τε βέλος.
> Ζεῦ Ζεῦ, κάτωθεν ἀμπέμπων
> ὑστερόποινον ἄταν,
> βροτῶν τλάμονι καὶ πανούργῳ
> χειρί, τοκεῦσι δ' ὅμως τελεῖται.

> [This cry has come to your ear
> like a deep driven arrow

> Zeus, Zeus, force up from below.
> ground the delayed destruction
> on the hard heart and the daring
> hand, fulfillment for our parents]
> (ll. 380–85)

Zeus sends ruin upon the wrongdoer; but even so the act of vengeance will be performed. In murdering his mother, Orestes becomes, like her, a transgressor against whose impious hand destruction will be summoned from the lower world. Nonetheless he accepts the task demanded of him. Syntactical irregularity heightens the ominous effect. An idea is almost stated, then suddenly replaced by vaguer formulation. The vocative Ζεῦ and its modifying participle are left without a verb. Orestes seems to break off because he shrinks from a more direct imprecation against his mother. What this strophe merely implies is stated with force and clarity in lines 434–38; there Orestes affirms his willingness to murder Clytemnestra even should it cost his life.

In the strophe which follows Orestes' ambiguous resolve to bring about "fulfillment for the parent," be it mother, father, or both at once, the Chorus attempt to focus his attention on Clytemnestra. The vague plural previously used is now discarded; they speak of a man struck down, a woman slain (ll. 387–89). For the first time Clytemnestra is differentiated from Aegisthus, her death for the first time explicitly included in the prayer for vengeance. From this moment on Aegisthus fades into the background.

### HARM FROM THE PARENT

In line 419 a similar plural occurs, this time a less equivocal periphrasis for "mother." The latter follows three lines later, its first appearance in the commos. It is used at a crucial point: in a strophe which closes the first part of the lyric and leads Orestes to new decision. Lines 418–22 act as a bridge between the two sections, rounding off the one in words reminiscent of the first strophic pair, opening the other with an introduction of what is to come.

Orestes began the commos with a question:

> ὦ πάτερ αἰνόπατερ, τί σοι
> φάμενος ἢ τί ῥέξας
> τύχοιμ' ἄν.

"Father, what's the right word to speak, what act perform, that I may reach you?" (ll. 315–17). In the first antistrophe Electra supplies the answer:

> Ηλ. κλῦθί νυν, ὦ πάτερ, ἐν μέρει
> πολυδάκρυτα πέθη.

"Father, hear each lament his grief in turn." Both are recalled in lines 418–19 when Electra asks: "What's the right word to speak? Sorrows suffered from one who gave us birth?"

> τί δ᾽ ἂν <u>φάντες τύχοιμεν</u>; ἢ τάπερ
> πάθομεν ἄχεα πρός γε τῶν τεκομένων.

Two interpretations of this line are possible. Electra's question, like that of Orestes in the first strophe, may be addressed to their father. . . . However, there are obstacles in the way of unconditional acceptance. This entire section is sprinkled with verbs in the second person (ll. 439, 443, 450, 451). Two of these might be addressed to Agamemnon or Orestes, but the other two can only be addressed to Orestes. Accordingly, several scholars follow Wilamowitz in assuming that lines 418–19 and the narrative which follows are directed not at Agamemnon but at his avenger. Electra's question in line 418, like the preceding choral strophe, is motivated by the note of hopelessness on which Orestes' strophe ended (πᾶ / τις τράποιτ᾽ ἂν, ὦ Ζεῦ; 408–9).

These two interpretations should be joined together. In form and content the second part of the commos resembles the ritual of an anakletikos hymnos; however, the old form is put to new purpose. Motifs associated with invocation to the dead are used here to rouse the living. The question "With what words would we attain our end?", the narration of misfortunes past and present, do recall the opening appeal to Agamemnon, do anticipate the trimeters which follow. Both question and narrative are now directed at the avenger rather than the dead man to be avenged. After the commos full regard can be turned to Agamemnon because the spirit of wrath has been conjured up with Orestes. The indirection of the commos, its dual purpose, gives way to the directness of a traditional invocation with single aim.

The lines that follow Electra's question present a confusing number of possibilities. As always, interpretation should embrace the entire range of significance, not reduce the passage to a single meaning arrived at by the process of elimination.

τί δ᾽ ἂν φάντες τύχοιμεν; ἢ τάπερ
πάθομεν ἄχεα πρός γε τῶν τεκομένων;
πάρεστι σαίνειν, τὰ δ᾽ οὔτι θέλγεται.
λύκος γὰρ ὥστ᾽ ὠμόφρων ἄσαντος ἐκ
ματρός ἐστιν θυμός.

The following is a literal, if unattractive, translation: "What can we say to gain our end? Should we tell of harm suffered from the very ones who gave us birth? It's possible to fawn but these things are not charmed away; for like a wolf cruel and unfawning (or unable to be fawned upon) is that nature from the mother" (ll. 418–22).

This might mean that though Clytemnestra fawn upon her children, attempting to allay their anger, she cannot appease them. From her they have inherited that wolflike nature which cannot be appeased; the nature that drove her to avenge Iphigenia's death drives them to avenge the murder of Agamemnon. Or it could mean that the children may fawn and cringe before their mother, pretending to aquiesce, as Electra has until this moment. But the wrongs done them are still resented, do not disappear from memory like magic. A wolfish nature, their true heritage, lurks unfawning behind words of flattery. And such was their mother's behavior toward Agamemnon. The confusion here, created by omission of a personal pronoun, abetted by an adjective either active or passive, brings out the likeness of child to parent. They may fawn, she may fawn; theirs is her nature which will not fawn, cannot be fawned upon.

Electra's words also suggest another, more general meaning. Like the lion parable which it resembles, this passage is a statement on the theme of guilt and retribution handed down to child from parent. πρός [prós] with the genitive, especially the genitive of such a word as τεκό-μενοι [tekómenoi], suggests origin or descent. The woes which Electra and Orestes suffer "from their parents" can no more be smoothed or charmed away (θέλγεται) than blood once spilled can be called back by charm or physician's remedy. From their parents they have inherited this dilemma: the obligation to take vengeance for Agamemnon's murder, itself in part a payment for the crime of Atreus. Thus the ἄχεα πρός γε τῶν τεκομένων [áchea prós ge tōv tekménōv (harm suffered from the very ones who gave us birth)] can connote the necessity of punishment and crime passed from one generation to the next.

At the close of the prologue Orestes was finally moved to pray for vengeance when he caught sight of Electra, her sorrow striking even amid a throng of black-robed women. And in the commos it is Electra who leads Orestes to join the figure of his mother with the murderess of his father. The word thus far avoided in the commos, the thought avoided from the opening of the play, are brought at last into the open. The strophes of Electra build to a crescendo: from the periphrasis τῶν τε-κομένων in 419 to ἐκ ματρός . . . θυμός in 421–22, ending ἰὼ ἰὼ δαῖα πάντολμε / μᾶτερ [Tōn tekomévōn (Of the parents) in 419 to ek matrós . . . Thumós (that nature from the mother) in 421–22 ending ìo ìo daîa Pántolme / mâter (Oh! Oh! Dire, dreadful shameless mother)] (ll. 429–430). In the following strophe Orestes repeats his resolve to take vengeance, a resolve for the first time directed against Clytemnestra alone, now no longer coupled with Aegisthus. Yet even so he refrains from the word "mother"; it echoes from Electra's apostrophe a few lines before. The vocative μᾶτερ [mâter], the second-person verb which his sister used, is softened by Orestes to a verb in the third person, its subject merely "she."

Orestes does not speak the word itself until that final moment of hesitancy when thought must be translated into action. Aegisthus slain, he confronts Clytemnestra and looks upon the face of matricide. At the sight he backs away, turning to Pylades with τί δράσω; μητέρ' αἰδεσθῶ κτανεῖν [What shall I do? Be ashamed to kill my mother?] (l. 899). Like the long-silent figures for which Aeschylus was famous, Orestes' long avoidance and final utterance of this word at this moment are eloquent. That is the climax toward which the commos builds. Indecision, dread, and new resolve are here openly expressed. In the commos they are communicated indirectly by ritual motifs of uncertainty and despair, by the structure of the lyric, and by Orestes' inability to use a word conspicuous in its absence.

## PARENT OF THE CHILD

Discussion of periphrases like τοκεῖς and τεκόμενοι has thus far been limited to significance in the context of the play. It remains to explore their meaning within the context of the trilogy. Substantives from the root τίκτω occur three times in the commos (πατέρων τε καὶ τε-κόντων, l. 329; τοκεῦσι, l. 385; τῶν τεκομένων, l. 419), their use unusual each time. These words are "significant" in the sense that they relate to a theme developed in the following play. The passages in which they occur should therefore be studied as a part of this development.

In the trial scene of *Eumenides,* Apollo ends the cycle of crime born from crime (φιλεῖ δὲ τίκτειν ὕβρις, *Agamemnon,* l. 763) with an argument which plays on the words for child and parent:

> οὐκ ἔστι μήτηρ ἡ κεκλημένου τέκνου
> τοκεύς, τροφὸς δὲ κύματος νεοσπόρου·
> τίκτει δ᾽ ὁ θρῴσκων.
>
> (ll. 658–60)

"The mother is not progenitor of what is called her progeny, but nurse of the new-sown seed. He procreates it who impregnates her." There is double wordplay here. In the plural τοκεύς designates both parents; the singular is used of the father only. Apollo exploits this usage to indicate that the mother's role is subordinate, the title "parents" being derived from a name applied to the male parent alone. Further, the words for child and parent, here juxtaposed, are from the same root. τοκεὺς τίκτει τέκνον [Tokeùs Tíktei Téknon]: it is the begetter who gives his name to the child begotten, not the mother.

The trial scene in general and this argument in particular are something of a puzzle. Is Apollo to be taken seriously or is this pure sophistry, mere paradox, introduced *pour épater le bourgeois* then as now? The view advanced by Apollo has other renowned adherents, foremost among them Anaxagoras and Aristotle. When Athena casts the deciding vote, she gives her motherless birth, her masculine nature, as reason for holding the man in higher honor than the wife. It is thought that she thus reinforces Apollo's argument by an appeal to the status of women in fifth-century Athens. Does Aeschylus then subscribe wholeheartedly to the theory advanced by Apollo, taken up by Athena? Does he desire his audience to do so? Such questions are part of a larger issue involving the entire trial; they can, however, be treated here with profit. . . .

To what extent does the argument of Apollo represent the thought of Aeschylus? It is, of course, impossible to answer with anything approaching certainty. However, recurrent use of words from the root τεκ- calls attention to the shaky foundation on which the argument, as presented here, is based. It is no less one-sided than Apollo's total rejection of the Erinyes and the justice they uphold. The paradox of Dike continues; there is right and wrong on both sides. Solution of the problem comes not from adherence to one view but from reconciliation of the two that each may exercise its proper social function. It is an oversimplification to assert, as Solmsen does, that Aeschylus believes in the natural superiority of the male and finds a solution "with the help of dialectical reasoning." The old order, the female element, the irrational, whatever term finds current favor: this force is dangerous because so powerful. More than that, it is indispensable and becomes the foundation on which the new order rests. . . .

[O]nce the thematic significance of such words as τοκεύς [Tokeús] and τίκτω [Tíktō] is established, one can perceive another level of meaning in the passages where they occur.

The Chorus assure Orestes that "just lament for fathers and for parents (πατέρων τε καὶ τεκόντων [Patérōn te kaì Tekóntōn]) seeks its object out" (ll. 329–30). Some commentators regard πατέρων τε καὶ τεκόντων as redundancy. Verrall and Groeneboom suggest that πατέρων [Patérōn] has here the wider sense of "ancestors"; it is then supplemented by the more specific "and parents in particular." Viewed as part of a theme developed through repetition of significant words, the phrase has another connotation. "Fathers and progenitors" because the father is the true parent to whom alone the child is linked by ties of blood, to whom he owes his first allegiance. In this strophe the Chorus also address Orestes as τέκνον [Téknon]. Thus the wordplay with which Apollo wins Orestes' acquittal for his crime is suggested as the Chorus begin to urge him toward performance of that crime.

In line 385 Orestes utters the ambiguous "Even for parents (or for the parent) there will be fulfillment." The plurality of possible meanings in this line raises the question of parentage. Orestes promises fulfillment to the author of his being. Does this refer to the father who alone, as sole true parent, merits the title τοκεύς [Tokeús], alone can claim payment (τελεῖται) for the debt of kinship? Is it the mother, herself parent of that crime Orestes must commit, she to whom he owes his serpent nature? The use of the plural which means "both parents" in a context where it is likely to be taken as a "poetic" plural referring either to the father alone or to the mother focuses attention on one or the other as *the* parent. In such a way this line prepares for the conflict of *Eumenides*.

In lines 418–19 Electra speaks of afflictions which proceed from τῶν τεκομένων [Tôn Tekoménōn]. Again a plural designates one parent, a plural which could be masculine or feminine. And as is fixed by the lines which follow, here the "parents" are the mother. (This is the meaning uppermost since it depends on the immediate context.) Inheritance from her is emphasized more strongly still: by λύκος γὰρ ὥστ . . . ἐκ / ματρός ἐστι θυμός: "wolflike . . . is the spirit from our mother." In the son the mother's spirit is reborn; her crime engenders the necessity of like crime to which her child falls heir. This is the portent of Clytemnestra's dream:

herself a serpent she has borne a serpent. This is the lesson of the lion parable: from one impious act is born another, a child like to its parent (*Agamemnon*, ll. 750–71). Orestes truly is his mother's son, his act of vengeance offspring of her own.

# The Dynamics of Misogyny: Myth and Mythmaking in the *Oresteia*

*Froma I. Zeitlin*

The *Oresteia* occupies a privileged position in any examination of the Greek mind and spirit and stands as one of those monumental works of art which transcend their aesthetic values, for it gives voice and form to the social and political ideology of the period at the same time as it actively shapes the collective fantasies of its audience with its own authoritative vision. By taking as his subject a dynastic myth known to us from the very beginning of Greek literature and transforming it into a wide-ranging myth of origins, Aeschylus draws upon his mythopoetic powers in the service of world-building. The last play leads us back to a reenactment of the cosmic struggle between Olympian and chthonic forces, and the trilogy ends with two social but divinely sanctioned acts of creation: the first human court to judge cases of homicide and the new religious cult of the Eumenides. The *Oresteia*'s program is to trace the evolution of civilization by placing the *polis* at the center of its vision and endowing it with the creative power to coordinate human, natural, and divine forces.

For Aeschylus, civilization is the ultimate product of conflict between opposing forces, achieved not through a *coincidentia oppositorum* but through a hierarchization of values. The solution, therefore, places Olympian over chthonic on the divine level, Greek over barbarian on the cultural level, and male above female on the social level. But the male-female

From *Arethusa* 2 (1978). © 1978 by the Department of Classics, State University of New York at Buffalo.

conflict subsumes the other two, for while it maintains its own emotive function in the dramatization of human concerns, it provides too the central metaphor which "sexualizes" the other issues and attracts them into its magnetic field. This schematization is especially marked in the confrontation between Apollo and the Erinyes in the *Eumenides* where juridical and theological concerns are fully identified with male-female dichotomies. Moreover, the basic issue in the trilogy is the establishment in the face of female resistance of the binding nature of patriarchal marriage where wife's subordination and patrilineal succession are re-affirmed. In the course of the drama, in fact, every permutation of the feminine is exhibited before us: goddess, queen, wife, mother, daughter, sister, bride, virgin, adulteress, nurse, witch, Fury, priestess. Every issue, every action stems from the female so that she serves as the catalyst of events even as she is the main object of inquiry.

Viewed as a gynecocentric document, the *Oresteia* then holds an equally privileged position in any exploration of the Greek image of the female, the definition of her social role and status, her functions and meanings. If Aeschylus is concerned with world-building, the cornerstone of his architecture is the control of woman, the social and cultural pre-requisite for the construction of civilization. The *Oresteia* stands squarely within the misogynistic tradition which pervades Greek thought, a bias which both projects a combative dialogue in male-female interactions and which relates the mastery of the female to higher social goals.

But in the breadth of its scope and in the complexity of its treatment, the *Oresteia* moves out beyond the other exemplars. The diachronic sweep of the trilogic form creates a broad field in space and time for amplifying patterns and themes, while mythopoetic stratagems lend prestigious authority to dramatic enactment. The *Oresteia* expands the paradigm by incorporating other myths and mythic elements into a comprehensive frame of reference and transforms it by an imaginative synthesis which culminates in the creation of a definitive new myth. The trilogy looks both ways. It stands as the fullest realization of an attitude which from its first literary expression in the *Odyssey* is already associated with Clytemnestra. But by integrating the issue into a coherent system of new values, by formulating it in new abstract terms, and by shifting to a new mode of argumentation, it provides the decisive model for the future legitimation of this attitude in Western thought. It is the purpose of this paper to examine the *Oresteia* as mythopoesis and to reveal the strategies by which it achieves its aims.

### THE MYTH OF MATRIARCHY

The progression of events in the *Oresteia* is straightforward. Woman rises up against male authority in a patriarchal society. By slaying her husband and by choosing her own sexual partner, she shatters the social norms and brings social functioning to a standstill. Portrayed as monstrous androgyne, she demands and usurps male power and prerogatives. Son then slays mother in open alliance with the cause of father and husband, and mother's Erinyes, in turn, pursue him in retribution.

The dynamics of the process, however, are noteworthy. Clytemnestra, the female principle, in the first play is a shrewd intelligent rebel against the masculine regime, but by the last play, through her representatives, the Erinyes, female is now allied with the archaic, primitive, and regressive, while male in the person of the young god, Apollo, champions conjugality, society, and progress, and his interests are ratified by the androgynous goddess, Athena, who sides with the male and confirms his primacy. Through gradual and subtle transformations, social evolution is posed as a movement from female dominance to male dominance, or, as it is often figuratively phrased, from "matriarchy" to "patriarchy."

For Bachofen, as for many who followed him, this evolution represented a true historical development, and it was no accident that for verification of his general theories of the origins of society he drew heavily on ancient classical sources, including the *Oresteia,* and gave his different phases names drawn from Greek mythology. For the Greek mythic imagination is rich in projections of female autonomy and Greek religion is amply populated with powerful female deities who seem to antedate their male counterparts in the pantheon. The great Greek culture heroes, Heracles and Theseus, are aggressively misogynistic and each counts among his founding acts of civilization the confrontation and defeat of those woman warriors, the Amazons. Iconographically, the Amazonomachy figures on the same level of significance as those two other great victories over the giants and the centaurs. The female, the earth-born elements, and the hybrid beast share the same associative sphere.

But matriarchy in the literal meaning of the term is not provable as a historical reality whatever the differences in social structure may have been between the inhabitants of the Aegean basin and the invading Indo-Europeans. Far more compelling is Bamberger's theory of the myth of matriarchy as myth, not "a memory of history, but a social charter," which "may be part of social history in providing justification for a present and perhaps permanent reality by giving an invented 'historical' explanation of how this reality was created."

From a cross-cultural perspective, the *Oresteia* can be characterized as an intricate and fascinating variant of a widely distributed myth of matriarchy, the so-called Rule of Women, whose details differ but whose general scenario conforms to a consistent pattern. Such myths are normally found in "societies where there also exists a set of cultural rules and procedures for determining sexual dimorphism in social and cultural tasks." Women once had power, but they abused it through "trickery and unbridled sexuality," thus fostering "chaos and misrule." The men, therefore, rebelled. They assumed control and took steps to institutionalize the subordination of women. The point of the myth is not the recording of some historical or prehistorical state of affairs, but rather that women are not fit to rule, only to be ruled.

While the simpler myth of matriarchy reads as a definitive masculine triumph which establishes the pattern for all time, the variations, repetitions, and frequency of the pattern in Greek myths attest to the continuing renewability of the battle between the sexes in many areas and circumstances. The conflictual nature of the encounter is consonant with the generally agonistic outlook of the Greek world, while the consistency of the portrayal of the woman reflects perhaps the deep-seated conviction that the female is basically unruly. The vigorous denial of power to the female overtly asserts her inferiority while at the same time expresses anxiety towards her persistent but normally dormant power which may always erupt into open violence. But the eruption of that force is not perceived as a purely unpredictable menace; rather it follows a discernible linear pattern that proceeds in conformity to its own particular "logic," its own dynamics, which arises directly out of this fundamental ambivalence towards women.

The central role played in mythology by male-female encounters attests to the significance and complexity of the problem even as the proliferation of versions indicates perhaps the impossibility of finding a satisfactory conclusion. In turning to Aeschylus to outline the version of this "logic" of misogyny operative in his drama—the dramatic sequence of events and the hidden assumptions that regulate this sequence—it is noteworthy that the poet must in effect invent his own solution.

The conjugal relationship is the focus of the struggle. Already assumed as the preexisting norm, it is not accepted in its current form by the female as an absolute imperative. In the *Oresteia,* wife and mother, Clytemnestra, repudiates it from inside the society, although it may be rejected from the outside, as the Danaids, militant young virgins, do in another trilogy. The ultimate goal of both trilogies is the female's full acceptance of the marital bond as necessary, natural, and just. In each case, the prior rejection of marriage leads to the massacre of the male, the corollary of which is the threat of extinction to human society as a whole. Clytemnestra slays her husband. Danaids slay their bridegrooms on their wedding night. The polarizing imagination of Greek mythic thought not only establishes a strong dichotomy between male and female, it also posits predictable behavioral responses at either end of the spectrum where female self-assertion on her own behalf is expressed only at the cost of annihilating the Other. We might perhaps speak of an "Amazon" complex which envisions that woman's refusal of her required subordinate role must, by an inevitable sequence, lead to its opposite: total domination, gynecocracy, whose extreme form projects the enslavement or murder of men. That same polarizing imagination can only conceive of two hierarchic alternatives: Rule by Men or Rule by Women.

The portrait of Clytemnestra in the *Agamemnon* specifically links her independence of thought and action with a desire to rule, an emphasis which transforms a personal vendetta into a gynecocratic issue, which presents the first motive as synchronic not diachronic with the other. Husband is also king, an economy which conflates the two social statuses and erases political and domestic distinctions, and permits the merger of personal revenge and political ambition. Clytemnestra begins, in fact, as woman in charge, for, as the Chorus remarks, she is entitled to rule in the absence of the husband-king (*Agamemnon*, ll. 258–60; cf. 84), but her intentions are to make that regency permanent and she assumes the stance of political *tyrannos*, an impression that is explicitly confirmed by both the Choruses in the first two plays. She does not rule alone, however, in a full gynecocracy, but the principle is maintained by the delineation of her lover and later coregent Aegisthus. He is the male who has already succumbed to female domination. He occupies the female interior space (*oikouros, Agamemnon*, ll. 1225, 1626), renounces masculine heroic pursuits of war and glory (*Agamemnon*, ll. 1625). He is only an adjunct to, not an initiator of the plot against Agamemnon (*Agamemnon*, ll. 1633–37; 1643–45). In his erotic susceptibilities, he is not unlike his barbarian counterpart Paris who also commits adultery with a daughter of Tyndareus. The subordinate male, the strengthless lion (*Agamemnon*, ll. 1224–25) is the only possible partner for the dominant female, and the Chorus contemptuously marks this reversal of roles by calling him "woman" (*Agamemnon*, l. 1625). And when he does assert himself by baring his own motives and flexing his newfound power, he himself conforms to the stereotypical male model of *tyrannos*.

Note too that Agamemnon must also be assimilated to the pattern before his murder at the hands of a woman. The prelude to his death is his defeat in the verbal exchange between himself and Clytemnestra, a debate which is specifically posed as a power struggle between male and female in which male eventually yields (*Agamemnon,* ll. 940–43). The cause of that dispute, the walking on the tapestries, is itself concerned with a clash in values, and Agamemnon's objections are based on his correct perception of the gesture as one appropriate only to women and barbarians. But he has already announced his sexual appetites by bringing back Cassandra as his concubine from Troy, while his yielding to Clytemnestra's temptation marks his secret affinity with the Trojan king Priam and with barbarian values of luxury and gratification of desires (*Agamemnon,* ll. 918–21; 935–39). This antithetical barbarian world is portrayed in the Greek imagination as the world of effeminacy and of sensual delights even as it is the world where, logically enough, female domination is perceived as a cultural reality and where the myths of matriarchy are most often located.

Clytemnestra fully understands this cultural dichotomy and reveals it in an oblique and subtle way. After Agamemnon has yielded to her persuasion and has entered the palace, she urges Cassandra now to come into the house and to accept her fate of slavery, and she supports her argument by allusion to a mythological precedent: even the son of Alcmene, when sold into servitude, endured his life of bondage (*Agamemnon,* ll. 1040–41). Heracles is identified not by name but only through his maternal genealogy, and his enslavement, of course, was to the Lydian queen Omphale who is everywhere in the tradition associated with the Rule of Women. In fact, one of the prominent features of the relationship between Heracles and Omphale is the terms of his enslavement at her hands which required him to take on the role of female, to wear women's dress, and to do women's work, as well as to serve as the male sexual object to satisfy the needs of the queen.

If Omphale is an archetypal exemplar of the Rule of Women, two other paradigms point even more directly to the same mythological construct. In the *Choephoroi,* the series of monstrous women recited by the Chorus culminates in a reference to the famous myth of the Lemnian women, so famous that their deed need not be recorded, but only the judgment passed upon it as proverbial for the epitome of evil (*Choephoroi,* ll. 631–36). The crimes of single women come first, Althaea (mother),

Scylla (daughter), and Clytemnestra (wife). The Lemnian allusion completes the misogynistic progression by moving from one to all, from individual transgression to a collective menace that wipes out an entire race. Moreover, by redoubling the example of husband murder which immediately precedes, it places Clytemnestra's offense (which itself has passed into paradigm) within the larger frame of the Rule of Women where female aims to annihilate male.

If the Lemnian women serve a programatic function in the *Choephoroi* as a justification for the murder of Clytemnestra, the Amazons assume that role in the third play where Aeschylus shifts the aetiological explanation for the name of the Areopagos from Ares' trial on that site to the battle between Theseus's Athens and the Amazons, worshippers of Ares. There the Amazons, the open rivals of men, had built their own city, had asserted their will in rival architectural and ritual structures (*Eumenides,* ll. 685–90). If in the *Choephoroi*, the mythological emphasis falls both on the murderous aspect of the female in domestic relations and on her successful vanquishing of the male with its predictable results, the other exemplar shows the Rule of Women as a political issue and celebrates its decisive defeat at the hands of Theseus, champion of male interests. Clytemnestra is no longer the point of reference as Apollo points out since she did not confront the male in open combat (*Eumenides,* ll. 625–28), and she is the threat from within the system not from without. The Amazonomachy in this context rather serves to demarcate the major substantive issue of Orestes' trial as a battle between the sexes. Moreover, the prior victory over the Amazons serves not only to foreshadow the outcome of the trial, but, by association, to invest the new defeat with the same symbolic significance and prestige as the earlier one. In the synchronic perspective, past, then, is paradigm, but if we shift to a diachronic view, the substitution of tribunal for warfare, of law for violence, indicates an evolutionary development and offers a new paradigm for the pacification of hostilities.

These three gynecocratic allusions, each allotted to a different play of the trilogy, and together forming a series of increasing elaboration and emphasis, mark out different aspects of the general pattern of the Rule of Women. The reference to Omphale implies role reversal and sexual bondage, that of the Lemnian women focuses on the potential outcome of the struggle as the destruction of male by female, and that of the Amazons points to the conclusion of the myth of matriarchy—the drawing of battlelines and the ultimate triumph of male over female.

In the Aeschylean version of the myth, the woman does not initiate the hostilities. She is spurred to retaliation by a prior outrage inflicted upon her by a male. Clytemnestra, enraged by the treatment of her daughter as a sacrificial animal, plots revenge and is reinforced in her resolve to kill her husband by Agamemnon's intention to introduce his concubine into the domestic space of the legitimate wife. The Danaids are fleeing their suitors who view marriage as acquisition, rape, and enslavement.

But the female response invariably exceeds the provocation offered by the male and creates a still more violent disequilibrium that brings society to a standstill. The havoc caused by the female in the first play of the *Oresteia* requires two further sequels to alleviate it, and the shock waves ripple out first to the city of Argos and then to the universe at large. In the *rhetorical* progression of the drama the crimes of the males of the house, Thyestes, Atreus, and Agamemnon, first fade into lesser significance and finally are mentioned no more.

In the *Choephoroi*, the uncanny power of the monumental androgynous figure of the *Agamemnon* has receded. Clytemnestra rules with Aegisthus over Argos, but she is now back in the interior of the house, not visible in the world of men and politics. She sends libations to the tomb of Agamemnon, but her action creates a ritual impasse since the wife who owes this duty to her husband is also his murderer (*Choephoroi,* ll. 84–100). This impasse is emblematic of the dysfunction of the social order under her regime, and she herself poses the problem which must be resolved if the social order is to be repaired and restored. The impasse is also manifested in the social status of the legitimate children: Electra, unwed, arrested in maidenhood, bound to the paternal hearth, and Orestes, an exile, as yet unable to cross the boundary to adulthood, a status contingent upon his assumption of his father's name and space. The house is shrouded in darkness, literal and metaphorical, the blood is frozen in the earth (*Choephoroi,* ll. 51–53, 66–67), and the children have a past but no future. That past, in fact, must be recalled and recreated in the long *kommos,* even as the free flowing of pent-up libations, tears, and verbal laments is the first symbolic step towards liberation from the suffocating spiritual and social deadlock of the current regime.

The only solution envisioned by the myth is the retaliatory defeat of this self-willed female principle whose potency is still a living and malignant force. And the myth proposes only one candidate for the task; the rules of blood vendetta exclude any other. Son must slay mother; father must be avenged, but in so doing, son's alliance with paternal power and interests must simultaneously be seen as repudiation of the mother. Mother must therefore be presented as hostile to both father and to son. In Clytemnestra's dream of the serpent at the breast and in his encounter with his mother, Orestes represents both himself and his father; he acts on behalf of his father but also on behalf of himself. For Orestes interprets his exile from the palace as rejection by the mother (*Choephoroi*, l. 912), and mother's hostility to her children is confirmed by her treatment of Electra (*Choephoroi*, ll. 189–91; 418–19; 444–46), by her call for a man-slaying axe at the moment of recognition (*Choephoroi*, ll. 889–90), and, above all, by the nurse who exposes Clytemnestra's hypocritical grief at the report of her son's death and who herself lays claim to responsibility for the nurture he received as a child (*Choephoroi*, ll. 737–65).

But in the *Agamemnon* the queen's primary motive was maternal vengeance for her child, Iphigenia; her second one was the sexual alliance she contracted with Aegisthus in her husband's absence. There the two traits of mother love and conjugal chastity diverge, are, in fact, antithetical to each other. Here in the *Choephoroi* adulterous wife is now fully equated with hostile mother. The faithless wife who betrayed her husband and has taken his usurper into her bed has now betrayed her other children to gratify her own sexuality (*Choephoroi*, ll. 915–17; cf. 599–601). The confrontation between Clytemnestra and Orestes is remarkable for the queen's mingled appeal of maternity and sexual seductiveness; the breast she bares to him (*Choephoroi*, ll. 894–98) has both erotic and nurturant significance. The gesture that momentarily stops him in his tracks is the source of her power over him, the source of all female power. It is the emblem of the basic dilemma posed by the female—the indispensable role of women in fertility for the continuity of the group by reason of her mysterious sexuality and the potential disruption of that group by its free exercise.

It is significant that the maternal role should be exemplified in the first place by the mother-daughter dyad, for that is a relationship from which the male is excluded, a closed circle in which his interference can only be construed as an invasion as the myth of Kore and Demeter demonstrates so well. It is essential too that the mother-daughter bond be attenuated as it is in the second play, where Electra is her mother's antagonist and her father's ally, essential too that the mother-child bond in the *Choephoroi* include both male and female offspring, although the emphasis now falls on mother and son.

The dramatic sequence of events in the trilogy suggests a linear chain of cause and effect. If the female overvalues the mother-child bond, her own unique relationship, she will, in turn, undervalue the marriage bond, which will, in turn, lead to or be accompanied by an assertion of sexual independence (free replacement of one sexual partner by another), and will be manifested politically by a desire to rule. The next step, paradoxically, will be her undervaluation, even rejection, of the mother-child bond, as in the case of Electra and Orestes. Child, in response, will undervalue and reject mother.

Orestes' victory over Clytemnestra does not, however, as in the more typical myth of matriarchy, result in the defeat of the female and in the curtailment of her power. Far from it. The murder of the mother evokes a renewed and redoubled power, exemplified now in a proliferation of negative female imagoes of supernatural origin. The Chorus in the *Choephoroi* had resorted to another mythological paradigm to exhort Orestes to action: he is to be another Perseus who will slay the Gorgon (*Choephoroi*, ll. 835–37), the archetypal myth on another level of masculine triumph over female. But the projected model is not fully applicable, first, because Orestes himself is given ophidian attributes, and secondly, because the serpent dead is deadlier still. The Chorus's exulting allusion after the deed to Orestes' liberation of Argos by lopping off the heads of two serpents (*Choephoroi*, ll. 1046–47) is instead an ironic cue for Orestes' first glimpse of the serpentine Furies. In this play, the Erinyes by their appearance terrorize him into frenzy and flight. In the next, they would annihilate him by absorption into themselves in an exact and retaliatory inversion of the symbolism of Clytemnestra's dream.

This final stage in the developmental progression, in fact, links together the perversion of both relationships—mother-child and female-male. For the devouring voracity of the Furies, the incarnations of Clytemnestra, who would pursue and suck the blood from their living victim, represents both oral aggression against the child they should nourish and sexual predation against the male to whom they should submit. Clytemnestra has banished both legitimate males from the house and bloodguilt infects the earth. In the case of the Erinyes, as transformations of Clytemnestra, the result of hypersexuality is sterility and death. The virginal Erinyes are barren and sterile and create sterility in all of nature.

In the primitive portrayal of the Furies there is a regression to the deepest fantasies of buried masculine terrors. They are *paides apaides,* children who are no children because they are old and also because they are children who have no children. They are shunned and rejected by men and gods with whom they have no intercourse (*Eumenides,* ll. 1033; 68–73). Daughters of Night, they inhabit the depths of the earth. Repulsive in physical appearance, they drip and ooze from every orifice; even their breath, their words, their thoughts drop poison (*Eumenides,* ll. 478–79). Their virginity is negative virginity as Clytemnestra's sexuality is negative sexuality, and in each case the fertility of the land is threatened (cf. *Agamemnon,* ll. 1390–92).

The pacification of the Erinyes becomes the ideological effort to solve the dilemma of the inextricable connection between female fertility and female sexuality, between female beneficence and female malevolence, for the equation of the female with sterility and death creates a new impasse that spells an end not only to society but obviously to life itself. The solution moves to repair the female archetype which has been polarized at its extreme negative limit in response to its rejection and denigration. The solution also establishes marriage as the institution that controls sexuality and ensures fertility even as it serves to assert the inherent subordination of female to male. For female dominance is expressed paradigmatically by the mother-child relationship—concretely in the *Oresteia* by Iphigenia's death as the motive for the female's attack upon the male and generically by the natural dependency of the male child upon the adult female. Patriarchal marriage is paradigmatic of male dominance including the primacy of the father-son bond in patrilineal succession and the primacy of the male in political power.

## II. Separation from the Mother and the General Pattern of Puberty Rites

In speaking of the myth of matriarchy and the general function of myth and ritual as educational tools in preliterate or traditional societies, Bamberger draws a parallel between the myth of matriarchy and puberty initiation rites which aim at detaching the boy from his natal household and his maternal associations and retraining him for his social and political roles. She points out that "this regrouping of adolescent boys with adult males is prefigured in some societies in myths foretelling the demise of female power and in the concomitant rise of male privilege. The myth of the Rule of Women in its many variants may be regarded as a replay of these crucial transitional stages in the life cycle of the individual male." There is, in fact, a close correlation between myth and ritual since in the myth men often seize the sovereignty from the women by stealing their sources of power, the sacred objects (e.g., masks and sacred trumpets), and making them their own exclusive possession, while one of the important events in the rituals of initiation involves the revelation of these same sacred objects to the boys and the explication of their meaning. But in these cases myth is prior to ritual; an event of the past supports and justifies the ritual and its message.

What we find instead in the *Oresteia* is the sophisticated interweaving and transposition of traditional motifs from both the myth of matriarchy and the ritual initiation motifs from both the myth of matriarchy and the ritual initiation scenario. Orestes, specifically characterized as on the threshold of maturity in the *Choephoroi* (1. 6), lives out the myth in terms that bear a remarkable resemblance to generalized and widely diffused initiatory patterns, but his own special situation now determines and directs the final outcome of the myth. Rather than following out a well-trodden path to adulthood as countless others would have done before him as we would expect of an actual cult experience, he must make his own way through an unprecedented set of procedures created expressly for him, and he himself must act as the catalyst that brings a secular noncultic institution into being. Likewise, the myth of matriarchy reaches its predictable conclusion but through a series of stratagems that combines the old and the new.

Orestes in the second play is the anomalous male, the logical counterpart of the anomalous female, Clytemnestra. Male activity is normally directed outward away from the hearth for external validation of prowess, but the domain which Orestes must enter is feminine space. If Vidal-Naquet's suggestion as to his ephebic status is correct, as I think it is, the inversion is still more precise. The boy, prior to his entry into adulthood, must separate himself from the attachments of home and childhood to serve out his military term on the wild frontiers, where he is situated temporarily in a savage state, in a liminal space as befits his liminal position. But Orestes, the exile banished in childhood by his mother, *returns* at puberty to his home, that space made savage and undomesticated by his mother's action in order to undertake the most savage act of all.

In fact, in order to effect that separation he must commit a crime, the crime of matricide, and far from releasing him from his mother and her influence, the Erinyes now sing a binding song over him to draw him into their domain and keep him there. Orestes' true initiatory experience begins only after his *second* expulsion from the palace in Argos and is terminated when, reincorporated into society in the third stage of the *rite de passage,* he returns to Argos now as lawful ruler and successor to his father. The overt mission of the *Eumenides* is to effect the salvation of Orestes. And that salvation is contingent upon his successful separation from his mother, in other words, upon completion of the enterprise undertaken by Orestes himself in the second play. The task now ascends to a higher level, to the level of both gods and city, even as the myth of matriarchy can only reach its prosperous conclusion in this new setting through a similar upward revision of its traditional terms. That is, the *Eumenides* must now once and for all establish and justify in abstract, theoretical, and mythopoetic terms the principles upon which the predictable sequence of the myth of matriarchy is based.

This shift to a more inclusive level of discourse is necessitated by the terms of the main preoccupation of the trilogy which reaches its fullest articulation in this third and final play. The primary issue in the *Oresteia* is, of course, justice. In its proper execution under all circumstances, matricide, the extreme transgression and the insoluble case, serves only as the means, the irresistible catalyst. Kuhns shrewdly observes that "Orestes cannot know that he is directed to act on behalf of a further purpose; he does not know that the crime is committed in order that it may be judged."

But by posing the son's action in separating himself from his mother as a crime, the issue of justice and the issue of the female are inextricably blended, for in the offering first of justification for matricide and then in its exoneration, mother is also judged. And she is judged on two levels: first, the woman is judged as wife. The crime of Clytemnestra (mariticide) is measured against Orestes' (matricide) and found to be more opprobrious: "For it is not the same thing that a noble man die, a man honored with god-given sovereignty, and at the hands of a woman at that" (*Eumenides,* ll. 625–27). Secondly, the Erinyes themselves, the first judges of Orestes, are also judged. Mother has been turned into vindictive and archetypal female. In Aeschylus's new genealogy for the Erinyes they are now daughters of Night, i.e., totally identified with the negative female principle. And they champion a justice which is judged blind, archaic, barbaric, and regressive, a justice which is to be superseded by the new institution of the law court in which they will in the future play a supporting not a starring role.

The problem of the female is posed in a new set of terms and the victory that is won is predicated on a social transformation of a higher degree. The *Eumenides* therefore is everywhere concerned with change and transformation on every level both for the son figure Orestes and for the mother. For the archaic mind, as Eliade points out, it is a characteristic belief that "a state cannot be changed without first being annihilated" and then recreated from the beginning. "Life cannot be repaired. It can only be recreated by a return to sources."

The first word of the last play of the trilogy is *"prōton,"* "first," as Burke puts it, "the final oracular beginning." The *Eumenides* is a drama preoccupied with beginnings, with origins. Its *mythos* is itself a myth of origins, of aetiologies, on both the secular and cultic levels, and it supports and redeems itself by reference to the ultimate beginnings. Again to quote Eliade:

> Every mythical account of the origin of anything presupposes and continues the cosmogony. From the structural point of view, origin myths can be homologized with the cosmogonic myth. The creation of the World being *the* preeminent instance of creation, the cosmogony becomes the exemplary model for "creation" of every kind. This does not mean that the origin myth imitates or copies the cosmogonic model. . . . But every new appearance—an animal, a plant, an institution—implies the existence of a World. . . . Every origin myth narrates and justifies a "new situation"—new in the sense that it did not exist *from the beginning of the World.* Origin myths continue and complete the cosmogonic myth; they tell how the world was changed, made richer or poorer. . . . This is why some origin myths begin by outlining a cosmogony.

And this is precisely how the *Eumenides* begins.

The opening scene, as many critics have noted is both paradigmatic and anticipatory of the ending of the play. The Delphic succession myth (a parallel to the evolution of power in Hesiod's *Theogony*) provides a direct mythological model for the transference of power from female to male. Although it would not have been inappropriate in view of the prevalence of serpent imagery in the trilogy to cite the traditional Delphic version of Apollo's acquisition of the shrine by dragon combat with the Pytho, Aeschylus has substituted an orderly and peaceful version of the succession myth in order to foreshadow the peaceful and harmonious ending of the trilogy. "For a thing to be well done, it must be done as it was *the first time.*" Here is true mythopoesis and a reversal of terms: a new civic world is in the process of creation and requires therefore as its model an alternate cosmogony, a new myth of origins.

By the terms of the revised myth, Aeschylus provides a paradigm of positive matriarchy that acknowledges the principle but relegates it to a primordial past that has been superseded. But by his other act of mytho-poesis, he presents the Erinyes as daughters of Night, representatives of a negative matriarchy that must be overcome. In the Hesiodic attribution of their origin to the blood of Uranus's severed genitals, they were also associated with vengeance and retribution. In their new genealogy as parthenogenetic offspring of Night, the principle of vengeance itself is posed as wholly female and female in its blackest and most negative manifestation. The new genealogy anchors them to a stage antecedent to the Uranian creativity of bisexual reproduction and the generation of regular nonmonstrous forms.

In this juxtaposition of two matriarchal representations, the Erinyes are invested with the symbolism of the dragon-combat mythology that was displaced from Delphic myth. The Erinyes' desire to suck Orestes' blood, to engulf him, paralyze him, and draw him down into the dark-ness of Hades, is consonant with the general pattern of the archetype. Earlier I remarked on the failure of the Gorgon-Perseus paradigm for Orestes in the *Choephoroi,* but that failure resides not in the misnaming of the monstrous serpent female, only in Orestes' inability to play Per-seus. Here the transpersonalization of the female dragon (*Eumenides,* l. 128), the archetypal encounter recurs, but will be transformed. For neither can Apollo reenact his previous victory over the Pytho, nor will Orestes himself play out the part of the typical hero and slay the dragon. Nor will the dragon truly be slain, but tamed; the act of domestication will be presented in collective, social, nonheroic terms, and violence will yield to open persuasion, *Peitho.* Yet with the gods as agents, the struggle is also presented as mythic conflict between chthonic and Uranian forces, between regress and progress, that resonates with the emotive power of theogony, gigantomachy (*Eumenides,* ll. 295–96), and dragon combat. The defeat of the Erinyes is already prefigured in the prologue by their temporary pacified sleep at the shrine (*Eumenides,* ll. 47, 68) and by their subsequent expulsion from it by Apollo (*Eumenides,* l. 179).

In the perspective of the myth of matriarchy, the Erinyes and their characterization conform more closely to the general pattern. For they are now a collective of females rather than a single figure, and their quarrel with Apollo turns precisely on the issue of usurpation of prior female power and privilege. But it is the conflation of the myth of ma-triarchy and the myth of dragon combat that invests the *Oresteia* with its most persuasive rhetorical weapon. For the Erinyes on stage not only serve as concrete embodiments of the metaphorical allusions to them-selves in the earlier plays, but as true primordial dragon figures, they also make visible the metaphors of female monstrosity which have been associated with Clytemnestra from the beginning. In the *Agamemnon,* Cassandra delineates her as Scylla, amphisbaena, and mother of Hades (*Agamemnon,* ll. 1233–36), allusions which proliferate in the second play with references to *echidna* (*Choephoroi,* l. 249), *muraina* (l. 994) and Gorgon (l. 835). The two strands meet in the ode on monstrous women in which the mythological women who slay men are linked from the first strophe with monstrous eruptions in nature on sea, on land, and in air, in which the human Scylla, daughter of Minos, recalls her homonymous monstrous counterpart of Cassandra's accusation (*Choephoroi,* ll. 612–22).

It is this rhetoric, in fact, which already in the first play, provides the yeast which transforms the shrewd political rebel into an archaic *daimon* that menaces the world with a renewed cosmogonic threat of total disorder and which marks the male-female conflict not as a feminine revolution but as a struggle between the new (male) and the old (female). Female is allied with the forces and values of the past not only on the mythological level, but, as the combat shifts from that of husband and wife to one of mother and son, it operates also on the personal human level. In the generational code, mother is anterior in time to son. In the juridical code, the ancient principle of the blood vendetta becomes fully identified with mother, for it was her championship of the priority of blood ties which led her first to slay the male to avenge her daughter's death and now both to pursue the slayer, the kinsman who shed kindred blood, and to refuse her son the normal passage into adulthood.

If the recitation of Delphic genealogy is a myth of beginnings, the second part of the prologue, Orestes at the shrine itself, presents another modality of beginnings directly consequent upon the first one. Orestes is seated at the *omphalos,* the navel of the world, holding suppliant emblems of white wool and covered with the purifying blood of a pig. As matricide, his condition symbolically represents his status of moral ambiguity, guilty and not guilty, polluted and purified. As neophyte, his ambiguity is emblematic of puberty rites everywhere. In a state of liminality, betwixt and between, he is separated from the world and not yet reincorporated into it. In the process of transition and change, he must go back again to beginnings, this time marked in the biological domain by the imagery of parturition. In fact, "neophytes are [commonly] likened to or treated as embryos, newborn infants, or sucklings by symbolic means which vary from culture to culture." All initiations employ some nexus of death and rebirth symbolism as a mark of a transition to a new state, but the imagery in puberty rites has special relevance, since the essential aim of the rite is to dramatize the biological life cycle by indicating the death of childhood and the rebirth into adulthood, a symbolism supported by the applicability, for instance, of the cutting of hair both to rites of puberty and to rites of mourning (*Choephoroi*, ll. 6–7).

Delcourt, in her *Oreste et Aleméon,* inquires, why the blood of a pig in rites of purification? And she suggests that its value lies neither in its sacrificial nor its lustratory functions, but in its close association with female genitalia. The pig, as artistic representations make clear, was held over the head of the subject who sits "like a new-born under the bloody organ which gave him birth. The blood of the piglet was only symbolically purificatory. The guilty was supposed reborn, and reborn innocent, from the mystic *choiriskos,*" and Varro informs us that the same treatment was applied both to homicides and to those who had been mad and were now sane. "Just as pollution is disease and disease is death, so purification is a renewal of life."

Orestes then is ritually reborn at the *omphalos* of Delphi, the female symbol at the center of a place whose name means womb. But this symbol has been appropriated by the male hegemony of the shrine which Apollo himself received as a *birthday* gift (*Eumenides,* l. 7). The implication of the scene is of rebirth from the male, a necessary condition both for Orestes' redemption from guilt and for his passage into adulthood as son of his father. Cross-cultural ethnographical data confirms that one of the most consistent themes of puberty rites is, in fact, the notion that the first birth from the female is superseded by a second birth, this time from the male. The initiate is born again into the social world of the fathers and is thereby definitively separated from the world of his childhood and his maternal dependence.

What is remarkable in the compressed symbolism of rebirth in this opening tableau is its double reference, for if Orestes' ambiguous presentation is attributable first to his liminal status as neophyte, it is also attributable to the nexus of guilt and innocence which proclaims him still attached to his mother (i.e., guilty) or separated from her (i.e., innocent). He can hardly negotiate the first set of terms until he has resolved the second. And this second issue which is, in fact, the primary focus of the trilogy, will be determined by the new Apollonic argument in the new juridical sphere that his mother is no kin to him, that he, in fact, is born from the father and only from the father.

The Apollonic argument then, is a restatement in another mode of discourse, of what has already been represented here at Delphi. Orestes himself is drawn into the Apollonic milieu and is assimilated, if obliquely, to the pattern of Apollo's own development which brought the god from Delos to Delphi, from mother to father. But Orestes' position still lacks the conclusive ratification of society and its gods. It is only a beginning, and one that must move him from Delphi to Athens, from isolation to community. And the process that will define him will be linked to the process by which society will define itself. In this double task which the drama poses for itself as a simultaneous reciprocal development, the action veers away from the sphere of myth and ritual even as it continues the impulse in a new and different way.

Orestes' experience continues to conform to the constellation of symbols and events that cluster about the pubertal initiation scenario. For in addition to the liminal situation of ambiguity and the recurrent imagery of birth, death, and rebirth, other typical features include: (1) ordeal, wakefulness, suffering, silence, isolation, wandering, and terror produced by encounter with the monstrous; (2) close connection with the deities of the group; (3) the presence of a male authority figure as guide, who dispenses the "arcane wisdom" or "gnosis" pertaining to social and political realities couched in mythic and symbolic form, especially theogonic and cosmogonic material, as well as "instruction in ethical and social obligations, in law and kinship"; and (4) the passive submission and obedience to that authority. The main event of initiation rites is, of course, the revelation of the hallowed traditions and the secret lore of the group upon which that tradition is based. Here in the *Eumenides* the revelation combines both old and new to formulate the future tradition, the foundation of which is the judgment by law and the definitive hierarchical disposition of male and female statuses.

In the *Eumenides,* the power of the mother is first drastically undercut and even denied by Apollo, who, as representative of male interests, logically champions the cause of marriage, but that denial is then mitigated by a limited restoration of that power through the intervention of Athena and the transformation of Erinyes to Eumenides. But Apollo must come first, to be superseded but not fully denied.

In the short view, Apollo's argument can be regarded as a sophisticated legal maneuver designed to get his client off on a technicality, or, in a more ameliorative reading, to break the impasse caused by the disparity between the Erinyes' absolutist and rigid formulation of the issue (guilty or not guilty) and the Apollonian defense of extenuating circumstances. In the wider view, the Apollonian argument is the hub of the drama, mother right vs. father right, old justice vs. new justice.

On the one hand, his method of argumentation is fully consonant with the archaic mode of thought which can only express change in status and attitude through total annihilation or negation of the previous position. He had already demonstrated the superiority of male over female on the sociological level by proclaiming that husband-king-male is more important than wife-queen-female (*Eumenides*, ll. 625–26) and by pressing the cause of conjugality over blood kinship (*Eumenides*, ll. 213–18). Now he moves back to the beginning to assert the primacy of the male through appeal to the primacy of the father. This he can only do, first, by the denial of the mother's role in procreation on the biological level, and then by resort on the mythological level to the denial of the mother altogether. The mother is only necessary conditionally in the case of a uterine association; where that association is lacking, mother need not exist at all. The denial of *matriarchy* is achieved by the denial of *mater*. The tables are completely turned.

On the other hand, this archaic mode of argument is presented in the service of a new synthesis in a new environment. To break the binding force of the symbiotic link between mother and child (best expressed imagistically in the circularity of serpent symbolism), Apollo needs a new forum, namely, the law court, the city's device which admits the use of logical argument and debate even as it establishes the right of nonkin to decide disputes among kin.

In this context of a founding act, the content of the argument is concerned with beginning again, expressed biologically as embryology, mythologically as theogony. The rebirth of Orestes into innocence and the birth of the law court and civic justice are confirmed by resort to the archetypal paradigm of beginnings. But the argument itself is a new kind of argument. In proposing that the father, the one who mounts, is the only true parent of the child, while the mother is merely the stranger host to the embryo, the passive vessel during its gestation, the argument draws upon the new scientific theories of the day. But even as the argument looks forward in its advancement of new intellectual trends, it looks backward in relying for proof of this contention on the mythic concept of Athena's birth from the head of Zeus.

The mythic argument is not just an exercise in logical absurdity which poses the anomaly as paradigm. It is a sound strategy (not only for the reasons outlined above on the nature of archaic argument) within the rules of mythic thought. Athena's birth is of founding significance in the creation of the world. In the terms of Hesiod's theogonic myth of succession, Zeus, by this act, puts an end to any threat to his sovereignty, by incorporating the principle of intelligence through the swallowing of Metis and making that principle manifest in the world through the birth of a child whose sex indicates that she will be no political threat to her father and whose filial relationship proclaims her dependence on the male. The mythic form his act of creation assumes completes the trend of the *Theogony* which began with Earth's natural parthenogenetic capability and ends with the male's imitation of her. The seal is set on the finality of the transition from female dominance to male dominance by overt male usurpation of her procreative function, the basic source of her mystery and power. That usurpation is consummated in the total reversal from female as begetter of male to male as begetter of female. But in the course of this transition, male generative creativity is displaced from phallos to head, or rather, put somewhat different, phallos and head are associated together.

This connection is precisely the basis that also underlines the "scientific" argument. For already in some of the pre-Socratic philosophers as well as later in Plato and Aristotle, seminal fluid is associated with spinal and cerebral fluids; the hypothesis is that semen is transmitted from the brain and the spinal column through the genitals to the womb. There is more. The major component of semen is *pneuma,* a foamlike airy substance which contains the seed of the divine. Originating in the brain, semen is responsible for endowing the offspring with the essential human capacity for reason, for *logos.* Seed of generation, of intellectual ability, and of the divine element in the human species, semen confirms the innate superiority of male over female. For Aristotle, "the male provides the form and the principle of the movement; the female provides the body, in other words, the material; . . . the male provides that which fashions the material into shape. . . . Thus the physical part, the body, comes from the female and the soul from the male since the soul is the essence of a particular body."

Here in the *Oresteia, logos* and *mythos* usually posed in two different modes, make an alliance and interact to support each other. This alliance is, in fact, a microcosmic reflection of the larger alliance between male and female, new and old, secular and sacred, on which the trilogy relies for its conclusion. Through the myth of Athena's birth, theogony is recapitulated now in the new embryology, championed by the new generation of gods in the interests of a new justice. If theogony supports embryology, it itself is reaffirmed through the authority of the other. Through this union of *mythos* and *logos,* a new mythos is engendered, one that mounts a final successful assault on the power of the female and brings a new ending to the myth of matriarchy. Bamberger points out that "from [her] cursory study . . . women frequently are subjected to harsh outside controls because of their putative immorality. . . . And so it seems from myth that less tangible forces than biology [her unique ability and her important contribution to group survival normally celebrated in female puberty ritual but overlooked in myth] were brought to bear on the subversion of the female sex role. . . . The case against her was made out to be a moral one, divorced from the biology that might have given her sex priority under other circumstances." Here in the *Oresteia* the attack is a double one—against the adulterous wife *and* the reproductive function of the female.

As Hillman remarks, since "embryology is a *logos* of beginnings, it will be influenced by creation mythemes," and "because theories of generation reflect the differences and union of opposites, these theories will be influenced by *coniunctio* fantasies. Perhaps still more fundamental are the fantasies which afflict the male in regard to the female when the male is observer and female the datum." And he goes on to point out that "we encounter a long and incredible history of theoretical misadventures and observational errors in male science regarding the physiology of reproduction. These fantastic theories and fantastic observations are not misapprehensions, the usual and necessary mistakes on the road of scientific progress; they are recurrent deprecations of the feminine phrased in the unimpeachable, objective language of the science of the period. The mythic factor recurs disguised in the sophisticated new evidence of the age." Apollo is the first to initiate this trend. "The Apollonic fantasy of reproduction and female inferiority recurs faithfully in the Western scientific tradition."

Here at its inception *mythos* still plays a determining role and the *logos* of scientific argument is still rudimentary; copulation is equated with gestation in a false analogy. But for *mythos* and for *logos* the true model is social relations, and woman's new reduced biological function is a sophisticated translation of her social function, ratified by god and science. It is the patent absurdity of Apollo's argument that offends our own fully developed scientific sensibilities, not the principle itself of biology (false or true) as a justification of ideology. The issue of whether anatomy is destiny is still very much alive.

The very terms of Apollo's argument bring together phallus and head in still another way, for the ending of the trilogy is also concerned with a shift in modes of action and behavior, as it charts a progression from obscurity to clarity. Representation of symbolic signs perceived as female activity gives way to the male *logos*. Repetition and incantation yield to dialectic. Even more, "this turning away from the mother to the father," as Freud observed, "signifies a victory of intellectuality over the senses . . . since maternity is proved by the evidence of the senses while paternity is a hypothesis based on inferences and premises." A whole series of antitheses form about the polarization of male and female roles which can be tabulated as follows (although not all of them are treated in this essay):

| Male | Female |
|---|---|
| Apollo | Erinyes |
| Olympian | Chthonic |
| Unbinding (will; salvation) | Bind ("Fate"; binding song) |
| Marriage (nonkin) | Kinship |
| Father | Mother |
| Law (court) | Ritual (altar) |
| Intention | Act |
| Odd (three; trilogy) | Even (two, tie, *lex talionis*) |
| Center | Limit (frontier, interior) |
| Greek | Barbarian |
| City | House |
| CULTURE | NATURE |
| Future (young) | Past (old) |
| Order | Chaos |
| Rule | Unruly (misrule) |
| Above | Below |
| Head-Phallos | Belly-Womb |
| Active | Passive |
| Creativity | Fertility |
| Reason | Unreason (sexuality; passion) |
| Light | Dark |
| Life | Death |
| Clarity (plain speaking) | Obscurity (riddle) |
| Intellect (paternity, inference) | Senses (maternity, representation) |
| Positive | Negative |

If the birth of Athena is necessary for Apollo's synthesis and Orestes' reincorporation into community, her pedigree and status are necessary for reaching any workable solution to the problem of the female who resists the encroachment on her prerogatives. Androgynous compromise, Athena is the benevolent answer to her opposite and doublet, Clytemnestra. Female born of male, she can ally herself with male interests and still display positive nurturant behavior. As deified female, child of Zeus, she can initiate authoritative religious and social change. But as female herself, she can serve too as model of the female. But not alone. For Athena and the Erinyes whom she has placated are not separate entities but complements, each of them virgins, each now charged with the fostering of the group, and together representing the reconciliation of the positive and negative elements of the female archetype on the transpersonal level. Both agree that female will be subordinate to male within the family in patriarchal marriage and that the family itself will be subordinate to the city. Both in turn shower the city with blessings of prosperity and fertility. Each is content with daughter status, for the father-daughter relationship is the purest paradigm of female dependence, while the oxymoron of virginal maternity promises fertility without its dangerous corollary of sexuality. Mother is denied but not denied.

Orestes had denied his mother by the act of matricide and sought a new birth at the male-centered *omphalos* of Delphi. That new birth was just a beginning that sent him further to another altar, Athena's altar, upon which he sat, embraced her image, and held on tight. She provided him with the salvation he had sought. The positive maternal figure, in fact, restored him to his father and freed him to claim his social and political identity based on a new embryology and a traditional theogony. Like Athena, he now belongs wholly to his father.

In the double movement of this last play, Aeschylus modifies and diminishes the role of Delphic Apollo as the sole arbiter of the Orestean dilemma in favor of a larger more inclusive transaction that includes the allotment of prerogatives to the Erinyes—their old negative ones of vengeance, which are now defined and limited for the city's interest, and their new positive ones of benison and fosterage. The Hesiodic theogonic model is still operative, for Athena is both *porte-parole* of Zeus and the living incarnation of the *nature* of his sovereignty and how he secured it. Her allotting of specific roles and functions is therefore a direct continuance of her father's work which was not to create the world but to organize and classify its components and to make accommodations between generations. If the *Oresteia* can be viewed, as I suggested at the beginning, as a gynecocentric document, as an inquiry into the nature and limits of feminine power, this last act completes the transference of the *political* power (along the lines of the myth of matriarchy), which

Clytemnestra had brazenly claimed in the first play, to the *ritual* power of the female exemplified by the role assigned to the Erinyes in Athens.

From the anthropological perspective, the solution is perfectly consistent with the observable principle of patrilineality in which the male "transmits membership in the corporate descent group," while the female transmits "mystic potentialities, powers, or attributes" through the uterine tie. From this same outlook, the complementarity of positive and negative femininity is readily understandable. As Harris observes, "the double association of women as mothers with life and nurturance on the one hand and with death and destructiveness on the other is certainly widespread and may be well nigh universal. . . . The mother-child nexus and other ties through women always and everywhere appear both bad and good precisely because they are at the opposite end of the scale from the authority of society." For Harris, this double association is confined to the two poles of Erinyes-Eumenides, while I would include Athena, the other and chief custodian of Athens, as the main representative of the positive side, the one who persuades the Erinyes to modify their malevolence. But Harris's perspective enables us to understand the choice of Athena to effect the pacification of the Erinyes, for if we follow the anthropological orientation, Athena is the truly positive female figure precisely because she has neither a uterine tie of her own nor does she herself create one. Free from any but symbolic maternal associations, she thus foreswears any matriarchal projects. In this sense, the *Oresteia* also judges and justifies Athena.

Oddly enough, the androgynous woman in power does not disappear but is reasserted and reaffirmed in her divine counterpart. The displacement of the issue upwards in this last play avoids the specifically human dilemma of the female in her dual role of mother (power) and wife (deference). It also effectively removes the psychological issue from the human dilemma of a son who has killed his own mother by defining it as a social and cosmic problem and quite literally putting it in the laps of the gods. Only they can free him (as far as it is intellectually possible) from the irrefutable and often anguished fact of human existence that man is from woman born.

In the end, this new Aeschylean myth, like all myths, as Lévi-Strauss says, "perhaps explains nothing and does no more than displace the difficulty, but by displacing it, it appears at least to mitigate any logical scandal." But Lévi-Strauss is interested in defining the objective functions of myth and mythmaking in a society, not in confronting the potentially dysfunctional properties of myth for legitimating social and political ideology whose mythic basis is neither recognized nor acknowledged. Psychic impulses compel the creation of the myth, but once objectified and projected outward, the myth reinforces, legitimates, and even influences the formation of those impulses by the authoritative power of that projection, especially when it is embedded in a magisterial work of art. There is a continuing reciprocity between the external and internal, between individual psyche and collective ideology, which gives myth its dynamic life far beyond the static intellectual dimension. By uncovering the apparent "logic" that informs the myth, we can both acknowledge the indispensable role of myth and mythmaking for human cognition and at the same time lay bare the operations by which it organizes and manipulates reality.

# Hunting and Sacrifice in Aeschylus's *Oresteia*

*Pierre Vidal-Naquet*

The *Oresteia* begins with the appearance of a beacon which has been carried from the destroyed city of Troy to Mycenae, to bring about "light in the darkness" and "the return of summer in mid-winter," but which in fact heralds events that are the opposite to what they seem. The trilogy ends with a nocturnal procession "by the light of dazzling torches" (φέγγει λαμπάδων σελασφόρων) whose brilliance, this time, is not deceptive but sheds light upon a reconciled universe—though this does not mean, of course, a universe free from all tensions. As a result of the tragic action disorder gives way to order among the gods both young and old whose quarrels are mentioned at the outset of the *Agamemnon* in the shape of the conflict between the Ouranidai and who confront each other both before the tribunal of Athens and before men in general. However, from beginning to end two themes appear to run right through the trilogy, the theme of sacrifice and that of hunting. The *Eumenides* ends with the procession uttering the ritual cry women make when a sacrificial animal is slain, the ὀλολυγή [*ololuyē*]: "And now give forth the ritual cry in response to our song (ὀλολύξατε νῦν ἐπι μολπαῖς)." But the first sacrificial image appears as early as line 65 of the *Agamemnon*, where the entry into battle is compared to the sacrifice that introduces the marriage ceremony, the προτέλεια [*protéleia*], and immediately after this there appears the theme of the sacrifice which is unacceptable to the gods or, as it is sometimes called, the "corrupt sacrifice": "Feed your fire with wood from beneath and with oil from above, but nothing will appease the

From *Tragedy and Myth in Ancient Greece.* © 1981 by the Harvester Press Ltd.

inflexible wrath which falls upon offerings which the flames refuse to consume."

The image of hunting is no less in evidence. The omen which underlines the entire *Agamemnon* and not just this play but the entire past, present and future of the Atridai, is a scene of animal hunting in which two eagles devour a hare with young. As for the *Eumenides,* this play suggests a manhunt in which Orestes is the quarry and the Erinyes the hounds. These hunting "images" have been collected in a useful monograph although the scope of its analysis does not rise above a very banal literal level. The importance of the theme of the sacrifice was totally missed by even a scholar such as E. Fraenkel who simply speaks of a "travesty of ritual language to enhance a gruesome effect." However, during recent years it has been the subject of considerably more serious studies. In some, such as that of Froma I. Zeitlin, it has been a matter of pinpointing its various meanings in the course of the trilogy. In others, which are more ambitious and more controversial, attempts have been made to link the study of sacrifice to the whole of Greek tragedy, as in the work of W. Burkert and J.-P. Guépin.

Nevertheless until now nobody appears to have noticed that there is a link between hunting and sacrifice and that, in the *Oresteia,* the two themes are not only interwoven but also superimposed the one upon the other and that it would therefore be profitable to study the two themes in conjunction. And yet, after all, it is the very same characters, Agamemnon and Orestes, who play the role first of hunters and then of hunted, first of the sacrificers and subsequently of the sacrificed (or those threatened with this fate). In the omen of the hare with young devoured by the eagles the hunt is an image of a monstrous sacrifice, that of Iphigenia.

Greek hunting is a subject which has been relatively little explored. Yet it has a wide range of representational meanings. In the first place, it is a social activity which is differentiated according to the various stages of a man's life: thus I have been able to make a distinction and contrast between the hunt of the ephebe and the hunt of the hoplite, between the cunning, and the heroic hunt. But it is also something more: in a large number of texts from tragedy, philosophy or mythography, hunting is an expression of the transition between nature and culture. In this respect it is, surely, similar to war. To give but one example, when, in the myth of the *Protagoras* of Plato, the Sophist describes the human world before the invention of politics, he says: "First, men lived apart from each other and no city existed. Because of this they were destroyed by animals which were always and everywhere stronger than they, and their industry which sufficed to feed them was yet inadequate to fight against the wild animals (πρὸς δὲ τὸν τῶν θηρίων πόλεμον ἐνδεής). For they did not yet possess the art of politics, of which warfare is a part."

Equally close are the links between hunting and sacrifice, that is, between the two methods open to the Greeks of acquiring meat to eat. Does the one derive from the other, as K. Meuli suggests, that is, do the sacrificial rites derive ultimately from rites of the prehistoric huntsmen such as are still practised, particularly in Siberia? In order to prove his thesis on a historical basis, K. Meuli is forced to admit that the rites of the huntsmen passed through two stages before they became the rites of the sacrificers,—that the agricultural civilisation of the Greeks took the place of a pastoral civilisation which, in its turn, had derived from a civilisation based on hunting. Even if we were to accept these as proven facts, it is hard to see what they could tell us about the relationship between hunting and sacrifice in the case of the Greeks of the classical age, that is, in the case of a people who were not essentially a hunting community but who still did go hunting and for whom the hunt continued to provide many myths and social representations. In the circumstances even the historian—particularly one who is not simply an antiquarian—must engage in a synchronic study.

According to the myth reported by Hesiod, on either side of the altar upon which the Olympian sacrifice was carried out when the quarrel between the gods and mortal men was being resolved at Mecone, there were, on the one side, the inhabitants of heaven and, on the other, the dwellers upon earth. The gods received the bones and the smoke, the men the cooked flesh. The myth of Prometheus is closely linked to that of Pandora: possession of fire, which is necessary to the sacrificial meal, that is, at the level of the myth, simply to the meal, has as its counterpart, coming from Zeus, "the accursed breed and race of women" and consuming sexuality. This is the destiny of the Iron Age man, a labourer whose only salvation lies in working the fields.

The function of the hunt both complements and stands in contrast to that of sacrifice. In a word, it determines the relationship between man and nature in the wild. The hunter is first the predatory animal such as the lion or the eagle, second the cunning animal such as the snake or the wolf (in Homer, most of the hunting images are of animals) and third, he who possesses a skill (*téchnē*) which is precisely what neither the lion nor the wolf do possess. This is what is expressed in, among numerous other texts, the myth of Prometheus as described in Plato's *Protagoras*.

The act of sacrifice involves cooking; the sacrificed beast is, par excellence, the ox used for the plough. This sacrifice which, in an extreme case, is a crime and which is forbidden in certain texts is dramatised in the ceremony of the *Bouphonia* held in honour of Zeus Polieus, in Athens. Here the sacrificed beast, stuffed with straw, is harnessed to a plough while each of its "murderers"—from the priest down to the sacrificial knife—is "judged." But the link between the sacrifice and the agricultural world is actually far more fundamental than might be suggested by this festival which one might suppose to be of marginal importance. There is a fine archaic illustration of this: when, having exhausted their supplies, the followers of Odysseus decide to sacrifice the oxen of the Sun, what they lack are the necessary agricultural products. Instead of toasting barleycorn, they use oak leaves and, for the libations, water instead of wine. The result is a disaster: "the cooked and the uncooked flesh lowed as the spits turned." And yet there was an alternative to this impious sacrifice and Odysseus himself pointed it out: hunting and fishing.

In general, it is true to say that the hunt is the opposite to the classical Olympian sacrifice. We know that the sacrifice of hunted animals is a rare phenomenon (and this is all the easier to understand as the animal to be sacrificed must be alive). In general, hunting is linked with gods who are hostile to the city, the gods of nature in the wild like Artemis and Dionysus. Frequently, as in the Iphigenia myth, the sacrifice of a hunted animal appears as a substitute for human sacrifice, the savage nature of the victim to some extent mitigating the savage nature of the act.

Between these opposite extremes there are, however, intermediary zones which are used to good effect in tragedy. Euripides' *Bacchae* gives a striking description of the Dionysiacal omophagy (the tearing up of raw meat) which is an action in which hunting and sacrifice are confused. Pentheus is the victim of just such a sacrificial hunt.

I do not propose to list the passages of the *Oresteia* where sacrifice, hunting and occasionally fishing are mentioned but rather to emphasise the main themes in the three plays which we shall find to be contrasted with one another in some measure, item for item.

Let us start off with the Chorus immediately following the *párodos* of the *Agamemnon* and the account of the omen which appeared to the

Achaeans at Aulis. Even more than in Cassandra's great scene, the poet here "joins together distant memories and future prophecies" but, for the very reason that this is still early on in the play, all the hints here are far more veiled.

"Two kings of birds appear before the kings of the fleets, one entirely black (*κελαινός*), the other white of tail. They appeared close to the palace on the side of the hand that bears the lance, perched in full view, devouring a hare with brood unborn deprived of the chance of a last run, together with all its litter." Calchas immediately deduces that the eagles are the Atridai, that they will capture Troy, that Artemis, being insulted by the murder of the doe hare is liable to insist upon an even heavier ransom (Iphigenia) which will in its turn entail other catastrophes: "For a treacherous keeper guards the home, ready to assert herself one dreadful day,—Anger who remembers all and seeks vengeance for a child" (*μίμνει γὰρ φοβερὰ παλίνορτος οἰκονόμος δολία μνάμων Μῆνις τεκνόποινος*). It is thus that the cunning vengeance to be taken by Clytemnestra is predicted, in terms which can hardly be described as indirect.

Hunting terms and terms linked with sacrifice are here closely intermingled. The doe hare is "deprived of the chance of a last run" (*λοισθίων δρόμων*), and this is a technical expression to be found elsewhere. It is hardly necessary to dwell upon the fact that this doe is a hare, the prototype of the hunted animal and, according to Herodotus, the only species of which the female can conceive even while pregnant, such is the extent to which nature demands them as victims. The hare, then, is the antithesis of the lion and the eagle. Homer describes Achilles as follows: "He has the vigour of the black eagle, the hunting eagle which is both the strongest and swiftest of the birds" (*αἰετοῦ οἴματ' ἔχων μέλανος τοῦ θηρητῆρος ὅς θ' ἅμα κάρτιστός τε καὶ ὤκιστος πετεηνῶν*); he is like "the high flying eagle making for the plain through the dark clouds to snatch a tender lamb or a hare from its form (*πτῶκα λαγωόν*)," "the eagle, surest of all birds, the dark hunter called the Black One (*μόρφνον θηρητῆρ', ὅν καὶ περκνὸν καλέουσιν*)." But it is not simply a question of *any* hunt. As has been pointed out, a hunting rule mentioned by Xenophon recommends that "sportsmen" should leave newborn animals to the goddess: *τὰ μὲν οὖν λίαν νεογνὰ οἱ φιλοκυνηγέται ἀφιᾶσι τῇ θεᾷ*. The eagles' hunt is a hunt both royal and at the same time impious, for it trespasses upon Artemis's domain.

However, this hunt is also a sacrifice, as Calchas says quite plainly, fearing lest Artemis should insist upon "another monstrous sacrifice whose victim would be hers alone (θυσιαν ἐτέραν ἄνομόν τιν' ἄδαι-τον)," and the sacrificial element is emphasised in the extraordinary line 136, a masterpiece of Aeschylean ambiguity, which expresses Artemis's anger against "her father's winged hounds" (αὐτότοκον πρὸ λόχου μο-γερὰν πτάκα θυομένοισιν) and which means both "slaying a trembling hare and its young before their birth" and also "sacrificing a trembling, cowering woman, his own child, on behalf of the army."

Could one express the meaning of the portent more precisely than Calchas does? The prophet himself emphasises the underlying ambivalence. The favourable elements are clearly indicated. The eagles appear "on the side of the arm that bears the lance," that is, from the right; one of them has a white back and is a colour held to be favourable in religion. The eagles' hunt is successful. In one sense the hare with young is Troy, which will be caught in a net from which neither child nor grown man will be able to escape: Troy's capture will be a hunt. On the other hand the doe hare is also, as we have seen, Iphigenia sacrificed by her father. Artemis, the most beautiful one, the kind one (εὔφρων ἁ καλά of line 140) extends her dangerous protection "to the feeble whelps of the ravening lions as much as to the tender young of all beasts of the fields." Agamemnon is also a lion; Iphigenia is inevitably the victim of her father, whether as the pregnant hare, the eagles' victim, or as the daughter of the lion, Artemis's victim. Artemis, the goddess of nature in the wild, whose name is invoked by Calchas when he proposes the sacrifice of Iphigenia, only intervenes because Agamemnon, in the shape of the eagle, has already entered the world of wild nature. Moreover, well before the scene at Aulis, other litters of young creatures besides those of the doe hare had been sacrificed and devoured during the impious feast described in Cassandra's great scene. Later on, Clytemnestra says that it is "the bitter, vengeful spirit of Atreus" which has "struck down this full-grown victim to avenge the babes" (τόνδ' ἀπέτεισεν τέλεον νεαροῖς ἐπιθύσας). The doe hare can also be identified with the young children who were massacred.

The eagles are the Atridai, but the first of them to be mentioned, the black eagle, the dark hunter definitively devoted to misfortune, can be none other than the hero of the drama, Agamemnon. Is he not further on compared to a "black-horned bull"? The colour white, which is thus implicitly attributed to Menelaus, no doubt reminds us that the whole affair was to have a happy ending for him. Menelaus is the hero who survives in the satirical drama with which the play ends, the *Proteus*. However, to make the interpreter's task still more complicated, these *eagles* are also vultures (αἰγυπιοί) which the Chorus leader at the opening of the play describes wheeling above their deserted eyrie, claiming—and obtaining—justice for the theft of their little ones or, in other words, for the theft of the stolen Helen. Is this contrast entirely without importance? Did Aeschylus use two different words to refer to the same bird? This is what has generally been argued and it is true that the two birds are sometimes confused. Even so, it is strange that it should be the noble, royal creature, the eagle of the heights, which is presented as committing a horrible action and the ignoble creature, the carrion eater, which is seeking justice. Is not the vulture an animal which, quite unlike the eagle, is attracted by whatever is rotting, by the stench of corpses, and which dies when confronted by sweet-smelling perfumes? Is not this "contradiction" on the contrary one of the mainsprings of the play? The theme of decay is, after all, very much present. In Cassandra's great scene, the prophetess cries out:

> This palace stinks of murder and of bloodshed.
> CHORUS: Say rather that it smells of burnt offerings upon the
> hearth.
> CASSANDRA: It is like the waft that rises from the grave.
> CHORUS: You ascribe to it a smell that has nothing in common
> with incense.

In one sense the whole play is going to show us how this corrupt sacrifice, namely the murder of Iphigenia, follows upon others and brings others in its wake just as that monstrous hunt, the feasting of the eagles is preceded and followed by others.

The Trojan war itself is a hunt, and the Chorus describes "these countless hunters armed with shields (πολύανδροί τε φεράσπιδες κυν-αγοί)" who "rush in pursuit of the vanished trace of [Helen's] ship." These hunters are not "strangers"; they are simply identical to all those hunters dressed as hoplites or bearing a shield at the very least which are to be seen on Attic vases, contrasted there to the ephebe hunters who are naked. However, as is suggested, immediately afterwards, by the parable of the lion cub, these hoplite hunters do not behave like hoplites. We are about to pass from the world of battle (*máchē*) to that of the animal hunt which is wild and impious. The Herald says as much at the end of the speech he makes upon arriving back in Argos: "Priam's sons have paid twice over for their sins."

Clytemnestra had already suggested, cynically, that a war that did not respect the gods of the vanquished would be a dangerous war for the victors. Agamemnon later spells it out even more clearly when he describes the capture of Troy: the vengeance was ὑπερκότως [ùperkótōs], quite out of proportion to the rape of Helen. The hoplites, an ἀσπιδηστρόφος λεώς, an army of agile shields, are indeed the victors but these hoplites fight during the night and this is contrary to the Greek code of battle. The army, issue from the horse's womb, is the "consuming beast of Argos" which leaps forward and "like a cruel lion, has lapped up the royal blood till it has drunk its fill." The war, then, is a repetition of the hare's murder with the lion, another royal animal, taking the place of the eagles. Cassandra's great scene and the murder of Agamemnon in their turn repeat not only the sacrifice of Iphigenia but also the war and the death of Thyestes' children. It is hardly necessary to point out that here too the terms used are constantly those of the sacrifice and of hunting. Cassandra is a hound; Agamemnon is both a man struck down in a sacrifice which is all the more monstrous for being accompanied by oaths and the ritual cry of the family Erinyes, and at the same time an animal caught in a net, which is hunted down before being killed. He is victim both to Clytemnestra, the she-lion, and to Aegisthus, the cowardly lion which is also a wolf, (a creature both cruel and cunning in the eyes of the Greeks). He is also the sacrificer who is sacrificed and this hunt-cum-sacrifice is in its turn a repetition of the original murder which took the horrible form of a human sacrifice accompanied by oath swearing, and which was worse than a human sacrifice since it was an οἰκεία βορά [oikeía borá], a family feasting, the result of cannibalism in the home. The raw and the cooked, the hunt and the sacrifice—these meet each other at the precise point where man has become no more than an animal. The οἰκεία βορά is, in short, the equivalent of incest.

There is one remarkable fact which I believe confirms the above analysis: whilst, in the *Agamemnon,* the capture of the human being who is to be sacrificed is described in metaphors relating to hunting, the execution itself is usually described in metaphors relating to stock-raising. Iphigenia is first a goat, then a lamb; Agamemnon, whom Clytemnestra had described as a farmyard dog, just as she is the bitch, is caught in a net but slaughtered like a bull. This is another way of conveying the sacrilege since domestic animals which are, in effect, the normal victims for sacrifice, must give some sign to indicate their assent, and this is the exact opposite to death in a trap. Perhaps Euripides' *Bacchae* can provide us with an interesting point of comparison. When Agave returns from her hunting expedition, carrying the head of her son, Pentheus, she at first imagines that she has brought back from the mountain Dionysus's ivy wreath, "the blessed quarry," μακάριον θήραν, then that it is a young lion cub caught without a net, which is a real feat of hunting, and lastly, before discovering the truth, she imagines that it is a young calf, νέος μόσχος, which is however as hairy as a wild beast, ὥστε νὴρ ἄγραυλος. And so Agave praises Bacchus, the skillful hunter, the great huntsman ἄναξ ἀγρεύς. Where Dionysus has been so clever is in making Agave *hunt* her son even though she subsequently treats him as a domestic animal, without knowing how close he was to being this. What Agave does unconsciously is done in full consciousness by the hunter-sacrificers of Agamemnon. This wild beast which they slaughter as if it were a domestic animal is actually their closest kin, their daughter, or their husband.

Thus the *Agamemnon* ends in a total reversal, an inversion of values: the female has killed her male, disorder takes over in the city, the sacrifice turned out to be an antisacrifice, a perverted hunt. True enough, the last line, spoken by the queen, suggests the reestablishment of order but this is a deceptive and inverted order and is to be overthrown in the *Choephori*.

In a recent study of the first stasimon of the *Choephori*, Anne Lebeck has shown that the second play in the trilogy has not only the same fundamental structure as the *Agamemnon* but that it is its exact counterpart. Where, in the one, a victim is received by his murderer, in the other a murderer is received by his victim. In the first case the welcoming woman deceives the returning man whilst in the second it is the returning man who deceives the welcoming woman. This applies down to the last detail. The *Choephori* is indeed a true mirror image to the *Agamemnon*. However, as has been pointed out, there is a fundamental difference between the two plays. The theme of the "corrupted sacrifice" has virtually disappeared. Orestes does not make a monstrous sacrifice of his mother; he simply carries out the oracle's orders. Yet the theme has not disappeared altogether and the chorus of captives exclaims: Εφυμῆσαι γένοιτό μοι πυκάεωτ' ὀλολυγμὸν ἀνδρὸς θεινομένου γυναικός τ' ὀλλυμένας, "Let me at last utter alone the sacramental cry over the man struck down and his slaughtered wife." In the speech of Orestes, the blood of Aegisthus, but not that of Clytemnestra, forms a libation to the Erinyes, the deity of the underworld, and this is no sacrilege. In retrospect too we can see changes. Agamemnon is no longer the warrior caught in a trap and struck down by a sword avenging both the mistakes made in the Trojan war and the sacrifice of Iphigenia. The war is totally justified: "Justice has come at last; it has at last struck down the sons of Priam, and with heavy retribution"; and of the sacrifice of Iphigenia no mention is made, even by the queen. Agamemnon here becomes a pure sacrificer and his tomb becomes an altar (*bōmós*) like that which is raised to the gods of heaven; he has been a *thutḗr* a sacrificer to Zeus. Zeus will have no more hecatombs unless Agamemnon is avenged. In anticipation, the reign of Orestes is associated with banquets and sacrifices. The murder of Agamemnon has become hardly anything more than an abominable trap. Orestes deplores the fact that he was not killed as befits a warrior, in battle. When Electra and her brother invoke their dead father, Electra says: "Remember the snares of their new-fangled plots" and Orestes refers to "chains not made of bronze by which you were captured, my father." The poet mentions these "chains not made of bronze" several times,—when Orestes describes the machination (*mechánēma*) to which his father fell victim and when he defines his mother herself as a trap for wild beasts, ἄγρευμα θηρός. No more than a fleeting mention is made of the sword of Aegisthus which stains with Agamemnon's blood the net which snared the king and it is the actual net itself that is described as the murderer, πα ροκτόνον θ' ὕφασμα.

These remarks lead me to consider the central character of the *Choephori,* Orestes, who, although he is not strictly speaking a sacrificer, is a hunter and a warrior. What strikes us immediately with Orestes is his twofold nature: I do not refer here simply to the fact that he is both guilty and innocent, a fact which allows us to foresee the ambiguity of his acquittal in the *Eumenides.* The Chorus, at the end of the *Choephori,* does not know whether he represents salvation or destruction: σωτῆρ' ἢ μόρον εἴπω. But more fundamental is the fact that from the outset of the play Orestes is seen to have that ambivalence which, as I have attempted to show elsewhere, is the characteristic of the pre-hoplite, the ephebe, the apprentice-adult and apprentice-warrior who must use guile before adopting the hoplite code of battle.

Orestes' first act is to offer a lock of hair at his father's tomb, as a sign of bereavement. This offering of mourning (*penthētḕrion*) is, as the hero himself declares, a repetition of the offering made in thanksgiving for his education which, as an adolescent, Orestes made to the river Inachos. The lock is discovered by Electra and her companions and it leaves the leader of the Chorus in some doubt as to whether it belongs to a man or a girl. The truth is that it is quite possible to mistake Orestes for Electra who is his double. The sign of recognition between brother and sister is a piece of tapestry embroidered by Electra in years gone by and which represents a scene of wild animals, θήρειον γραφήν. And it is, precisely, a kind of hunt that they are about to embark upon together: an ephebe hunt in which guile has its, in this case, legitimate place.

There are many striking examples of Orestes' ambivalence in matters of warrior-like behaviour. Thus, foretelling Aegisthus's murder, Orestes pictures himself "enmeshing (his adversary) in supple bronze," ποδώκει περιβαλὼν χαλκεύματι. A net can be used for enmeshing but bronze is used for fighting. In one sense this hunt is really a *máchē:* Ares pitted against Ares as Dike is against Dike. However the guileful nature of this battle is also striking. Orestes says: "Having killed a revered hero by treachery, they (Clytemnestra and Aegisthus) must be caught and must perish in the self-same snare," and Clytemnestra echoes his words: "We killed by craft; by craft we are now to die," δόλοις ὀλούμεθ' ὥσπερ οὖν ἐκτείναμεν. Orestes depends upon "cheating Persuasion," πειθὼ δολία, and once the murder is accomplished the Chorus declares in triumph: ἔμολε δ'ᾧ μέλει κρυπταδίον μάχας δολιόφρων ποινά: "He has come at last, he who, fighting in the darkness, knows how to exact the punishment through guile." However, the very use of the word *máchē* alerts us to the fact that this is no ordinary kind of guile; the Chorus goes on to say: "Zeus's daughter, she whom men rightly call Justice, guided his arm as he struck," ἔθιγε δ' ἐν μάχᾳ χερὸς ἐτητύμως. When, at the beginning of the play, the Chorus is picturing the ideal avenger, it tells of a warrior armed both with a Scythian *palintonos* bow which must be drawn back to be strung and also with a sword "whose blade and hilt are all of a piece, for fighting at closer quarters." Orestes is to be both hoplite and bowman. Later on, when summing up, the Chorus proclaims that Orestes' victory—or rather that of the oracle—has been accomplished (ἀδόλοις δόλοις) "by treachery which is not treacherous."

It is the animal metaphors that must complete our study. It is said of Electra that she has the heart of a wolf and this places her on the side of guile and deceit. As for Orestes, he is a serpent, not only in his mother's famous dream where she sees him hanging like a snake from her breast, but also according to the definition which he applies to himself: ἐκδρακοντωθεὶς δ' ἐγὼ κτείνω νιν: "It is I who, becoming a snake, shall kill her." However, this relationship with his mother is reversible for Clytemnestra is herself a snake. She is the viper that has taken the young of the eagle; she is "a sting-ray or viper"; she it is who is the real serpent while the serpent Orestes is also one of the eagle's abandoned young complaining of their hunger "for they are not old enough to bring back food to the nest as their father did." Together with Electra he is seen as one of these. So it is that the image with which the *Agamemnon* begins reappears but now it is inverted. It is no longer the *vultures* which cry out for vengeance for the theft of their little ones but the young eaglets which are deprived of their parents. Yet Orestes is also the adult royal creature: in reply to Clytemnestra who calls her son a serpent, the Chorus declares: "he has entered the house of Agamemnon as the double lion and the double Ares," he is the very one who "with a fortunate blow cuts off the heads of the two serpents," Clytemnestra and Aegisthus. The serpents do, it is true, also make a reappearance upon the heads of the Erinyes. Thus the destiny of Orestes is not clear-cut: he is a double character, both hunter and warrior, serpent and lion. And in the *Eumenides* Orestes is to be found as the quarry in danger of being sacrificed.

I have attempted to show how, with varying degrees of ambiguity, the opposition between nature in the wild and civilisation is constantly present in the first two plays of the trilogy. In the *Eumenides* this opposition emerges quite clearly and even encroaches on the world of politics. The fact that we leave the world of men to see the gods come face to face with one another is only a matter of appearances. In the last analysis the play is about man and the city.

The speech of the Pythian priestess, in the prologue, gives an account of the origins of Delphi which is original to Aeschylus. It is a story of a "non-violent" succession (οὐδὲ πρὸς βίαν) in which there is no reference to the murder of Python. The deities that control the site fall into two interlocked groups: on one side is Earth and her daughter Phoebe; on the other Themis (Order) and Phoebus. Nature in the wild and civilisation alternate in the succession. The last incumbent, Phoebus, is supported by Zeus but he is accompanied from Delos to Parnassus by the Athenians: "The children of Hephaestus open up the way for him, taming for him soil hitherto untamed" (χθόνα ἀνήμερον τιθέντες ἡμερωμένην). Similarly, the invocation addressed by the Pythian priestess to the gods which ends, as is befitting, with an appeal to Zeus who guarantees the new order, clearly divides the gods into two categories. On the one hand is Pallas Pronoia, who opens the list at the end of which Zeus comes and, on the other, the "nymphs of the Corycian cave, the sanctuary of birds" which is also the lair of Dionysus "Bromios," the noisy one—"Let me not forget him" (οὐδ' ἀμνημονῶ)—the river Pleistos and Poseidon, the earth shaker.

The Dionysus invoked at this point is important to my thesis. He is a hunter who "led the Bacchae forth to combat (ἐστρατήγησεν) and prepared the death of a hare for Pentheus." This is the very death which the Erinyes are preparing for Orestes. In this way we are alerted to the issue at the outset of the play: the wildness of the world may be integrated and dominated by Zeus and this transition may take place without violence (as it does in the lawsuit of Athens) but none the less it meanwhile exists. To deny its existence would be to deny a part of reality.

So Orestes, the hunter in the *Choephori,* has now become the quarry. He is a fawn which escapes the net, a cowering fawn (καταπτακών), a hare whose sacrifice will pay for the death of Clytemnestra. Once again Aeschylus uses the technical vocabulary of the hunt. The Erinyes are the huntresses but they are huntresses that are purely animal. The wildness which was one side of the personalities of Agamemnon, Clytemnestra and of Orestes himself is unmitigated in their case. They are serpents and they are also bitches. Their purely animal nature is very strongly emphasised, by Apollo it is true, in line 193 and following: "You should make your dwelling in the cave of some blood-gorged lion (λέοντος αἱματορρόφον) instead of coming to defile others by inflicting your foulness in this temple of prophecy." At the capture of Troy, Agamemnon's army was also the bloodthirsty lion. The Erinyes even transgress the bounds of wild and animal nature; they are the "accursed virgins, the ancient hags from some bygone age whose presence neither god nor man nor beast can bear" (οὐδὲ θήρ).

Colour symbolism naturally plays its part in expressing all this. These "children of the night" who wear only black robes, whose hatred is equally black are threatened by the winged serpent, by the white arrows of Apollo. These deities also receive sacrifices which define their character equally clearly. The ghost of Clytemnestra reminds them of her offerings: "Have you not often lapped up my offerings, wineless libations, sober, soothing draughts (νηφάλια μειλίγ ματα)? Have I not offered up more than one victim at night, at your sacred banquets, upon the ritual hearth (ἐπ' ἐσχάρᾳ πυρός) at an hour given to no other god?" The composition of the sacrifice is significant: it consists only of "natural" products, of nothing which depends upon agriculture, and in the sacrifice the offerings are totally consumed. The Erinyes can claim the two extremes: what is "pure" and "natural" is also what is raw. They do not drink wine but they do eat men. Except with regard to the wine they resemble Euripides' Bacchae who feed upon milk and honey which well up from the ground and who eat the raw flesh of the he-goat before tearing Pentheus to pieces. The goddesses of the night also address Orestes with the following words: "There is no need for knife and altar, for my feasting shall be upon your living flesh, you, the victim fattened ready for my sacrifice." Here the antisacrifice is described for what it is, without the parody which was suggested by the murder of Agamemnon. But the most striking expression of all comes in lines 264–66: "In return you shall, while yet alive, quench my thirst with a red offering taken from your very limbs." A red offering, ἐρυθρὸν πελανόν [*eruthròn pelanón*]. The *pelanós* is a purely vegetable offering made into a cake or liquid. It is a *pelanós* that Electra offers up on the tomb of Agamemnon. A red *pelanós* is indeed a striking image of all that is monstrous.

The nature of the Erinyes is not altered when they become the Eumenides. As the goddesses of the night, they are the focus of the nocturnal festival with which the trilogy ends. They usually receive their victims, their sacrificial offerings, the σφάγια and θυσίαι, with their throats cut. Henceforth however, being the protectresses of growing things, they are entitled to the first fruits, "the sacrifices for birth and for marriage."

Far from being the deities of blood and of wild nature, they become the protectresses of vegetation, of agriculture and of stock-breeding and this includes both animals and men: "Let the rich fertility of the soil and of the flocks never cease from bringing prosperity to my city! Let the offerings of men find protection there also." There is a quite startling change in vocabulary from that of the hunt to that of agriculture and husbandry. The huntresses have a throne, ἕδρα. Athena requests the Eumenides to bear themselves as the φιτυποιμήν [*phitupoimēn*], the man who tends plants, the gardener who forks the earth in order to get rid of the weeds, the impure grasses: τῶν δυσσεβούντων δ'ἐκφορωτέρα πέλοις. Wild nature still has its share both within the city, since Athena herself takes over the "policy" of the Erinyes: "no anarchy or despotism" and since fear (φόβος) remains in its place there together with respect (σέβας), and also outside the city. Insofar as it forms a barrier: "the fire which lays waste the young buds shall not creep across your frontiers." Fury, "the bloody needles which tear at young guts" (αἱματηρὰς θηγάνας σπλάγχνων βλάβας νέων) and the world of animality must be reserved for war against foreigners: "I do not call it battle when birds of the same aviary fight against each other" (ἐνοικίου δ' ὄρνιθος οὐ λέγω μάχην). The shares of each kind in the different types of sacrifice has been determined.

# The Tragic Emotions in the *Oresteia*

*W. B. Stanford*

This [essay] proposes to illustrate how emotive methods are used cumulatively and on a grand scale by a master poet. The form adopted will be that of a running commentary focused on the expression and arousal of emotions in *Agamemnon,* together with some brief remarks on the rest of the trilogy. The editions to which I am chiefly indebted are those of Denniston and Page, Fraenkel, Groeneboom, Rose, Thomson and Headlam, and also Lloyd-Jones's commentary on his translation. . . . Readers would do well to have the Greek text or a translation with them for reference.

**Lines 1–39**   Here in the lively speech of the Watchman, Aeschylus, like a musician in the overture to a long and elaborate composition, briefly and for the most part unobtrusively introduces most of the trilogy's emotional themes. Fear is most strongly presented. Personified in line 14, and indicated by disturbed syntax in lines 12–15, it then yields to grief and groaning for the present state of affairs in the royal house at Argos. These unhappy feelings are momentarily banished by joy at the appearance of the long-awaited beacon and by the anticipated pleasures both of winning a reward for being the first to announce the good news and of welcoming the king on his return (*philía*). The sense of fear returns in the last lines, all the more ominously by being undefined as to its source. The final mood is that of the opening scenes in *Hamlet:* there's

From *Greek Tragedy and the Emotions.* © 1983 by W. B. Stanford. Routledge & Kegan Paul Ltd., 1983.

something so rotten—and fearful—in the State of Argos that even this bluff watchman does not dare to speak freely.

Other remarks of his prepare the ground for emotional responses later in the play. The description of the queen as having a heart that combines the hopefulness of a woman with the purposefulness of a man very quietly introduces the motif of perverted nature and monstrosity, which will swell to terrifying proportions. The symbolism of light (for joy) and darkness (for sorrow) will recur with many variations—dawn, torches, lamps, stars, the sun, shining justice and much else—all through the trilogy and will help to glorify its triumphant finale. The house, the accursed House of the Atreidai that stands like a silent character in the background of the action and looms up with terrible menace before the exits of Agamemnon and Cassandra, is mentioned five times (see further on lines 958–74). It is almost given a voice in lines 37–38.

We have here, too, a miniature exploitation of the technique of alternating emotions: suspense, fear, joy (perhaps visually expressed by a few dance steps at line 31 as well as by the cries of *ioú, ioú* in line 25), and finally fear again. An audience primarily interested in the character of the Watchman and the events he describes would hardly be conscious of these emotional sequences, but like a melody played quietly in the bass while the treble tune is kept dominant, they prepare the way for crescendos to come. The last warning "I speak to those who understand" might just be Aeschylus himself telling his audience to expect cryptic meanings in what follows: compare lines 144–45, 615–16.

**Lines 40–71** New emotions are mentioned briefly here—anger on the part of the Atreidai and the gods, pity for the robbed birds, *érōs* on the part of Helen "the woman of many men (or husbands)" in line 62. The note of grief at a disturbed home in lines 18–19 is re-echoed in the grief of the "eagles" (hardly vultures in this regal context) for their robbed nest.

**Lines 78–82** The cliché of the pitiable condition of old age is exploited emphatically in these lines. The Chorus for a moment provide a third object of pity after the robbed birds and (implicitly) the limb-weary warriors at Troy in lines 63–67.

**Lines 92–96** A different kind of torch, symbolizing thanksgiving, is lit. These torches are "medicined by gentle, undeceitful persuasions of royal oilcake from the innermost part of the house." This is strange suggestive language, possibly in preparation for the deeper symbolism of the torches to emerge later (see on 281). The word for the innermost part of the house here, *mukhós,* is used by Homer in his reference to Aigisthos' seduction of Clytemnestra in *Odyssey* 3.263.

**Lines 99–103**   The motif of anxiety becomes emphatic. The text of 103 is corrupt, but something like "insatiable worry and spirit-consuming grief of heart" seems to be indicated. This implies more than concern about the significance of the sudden sacrifices and illuminations. It expresses a deep-seated uneasiness of a general kind. Cf. on ll. 106–83.

**Lines 104–39**   Significant rhythm: after the conventional iambics and anapests of the preceding passages the dactylic hexameters and subsequent sporadic dactyls strike a chord which combines heroic *êthos* with oracular overtones, the first being apt for the picture of Achaean warlords on the march and the second preparing the way for the omen of the eagles and its interpretation. Lines 107, 116 and 126 can be scanned as a combination of a *dochmiac,* the metre of tension and strain, with dactyls.

In lines 119ff. a minor reversal in emotional direction occurs. The pitiful birds of lines 49–54 are replaced by birds which are emblems of savage cruelty: instead of losing their own young they are now destroyers of another creature's offspring (just as the Atreidai who were shown as being deprived of their nestling, Helen, in lines 60–62, will turn into murderers of another nestling, Iphigeneia, in lines 228–47). Artemis's reaction to the slaughter of the hare and leverets moves in two directions—pity (*oîktos,* line 134, first specifically named here) for the hare and both *phthónos* and loathing (*stúgos*) towards the eagles (ll. 134, 137). The refrain in line 121 begins as a lament for the slaughter of the animals and for the wrath of Artemis, but continues in lines 139 and 159 as a preparation for the more terrible child-slaughter that is to come.

**Lines 149–59**   After a repetition of the motif of waiting (suspense: compare lines 1–2) the Chorus introduces a tremendous personification of *Anger* in its most heavily charged form (*mênis*)—"Fearsome wrath that abides and springs up again and controls the house (*oikonómos*), deceives and remembers and brings vengeance for children." (A strong alliteration of *m* and *n* creates an aural climax for the word *mênis,* and the slowing of the rhythm at the words for "remember" and "anger" adds emphasis.) In fact this might almost be a description of Clytemnestra, as *oikonómos* strongly hints, since this word could also mean "house-keeper." She indeed embodies the abiding wrath of the house of Atreus, as the Chorus partly recognises in lines 1507–12. The harsh resonance of the verb describing Calchas' tone of voice as he uttered these ominous words—*apéklanxen*—both embodies the actual sound and suggests a *nomen omen* for the name, *Kálkhas*. Cf. on line 201.

**Lines 160–83**   Mainly unemotional. But, as Denniston and Page suggest, the reference to "this vain burden of anxiety" may refer to the Chorus's general uneasiness and not exclusively to [its] theological problems. In the phrase "Instead of sleep the travail (*pónos*) of remembered woe drips out in front of the heart" we have an ominous echo of the Watchman's complaint about his inability to sleep (through fear in his case). If we read *bíaios* agreeing with *cháris* we have an *oxymoron*—"forcible benevolence"—to express *taraché*. This quiet meditative passage provides a *calm before the storm* in preparation for the first major emotional scene (described, not acted) in the play.

**Lines 184–98**   *Taraché* also possesses Agamemnon. It is symbolized in the to-and-fro currents in the straits at Aulis—the notorious Euripos whose irregular tides are said to have baffled even Aristotle. The motif of weary waiting is stressed again in lines 194–98. As Lloyd-Jones observes, the syncopated iambics (ll. 192ff.) after the previous trochees effectively express the frustration of the delay. He also believes that the choriambics of lines 199ff. express the violent reaction of the princes to the prophet's words.

**Lines 200–204**   "The prophet clanged out (*éklanxen*) . . . ": again both the name and the harshly ringing voice of the prophet are embodied in the verb, but what he actually said is left to our imagination. We are told only its consequences, the tears of the Atreidai and the ensuing sacrifice. The *gesture* of the Atreidai, striking the ground with their staffs, seems to indicate that their grief is mixed with anger (cf. *Iliad* 1.245 and *Odyssey* 2.80).

**Lines 1–204**   Recapitulation. It may be well here to assess how skillfully Aeschylus in preparation for the Iphigeneia scene has gradually raised the emotional temperature—that is, the emotional temperature of us, the audience, not just of the people in the play. At the outset we probably felt some sympathetic vibrations of fear—and of momentary joy—with the Watchman, engaging character that he was. But they were hardly more than slight forebodings, though the words that the Chorus sang in lines 98–103 strengthened them. Our compassion has been mildly appealed to in the references to the robbed birds, to the warriors wearily battling at Troy, and to the slaughtered hare and leverets, as well as by the weariness of the Watchman at his long vigil. If we had been present at a performance with a powerful actor playing Clytemnestra we might have felt a frisson of fear from the mere sight of her as she moved silently across the scene at ll. 83ff., ignoring the Chorus's deferential questions (as I believe she must despite strong arguments against her entrance here). The other emotions mentioned—anger, *phthónos,* grief and *tarachḗ*—have had only a slight impact as yet.

Down to line 104 Aeschylus has not used any of the strong emotive techniques in his diction. He has been content to refer to the various emotions for the most part in cool language and conventional rhythms. But when the dactyls and dochmiacs begin to sound in lines 104ff. they mark an *accelerando* for our pulse-beats. The introduction of a lamentatory prayer in line 121 and its double repetition as a refrain—with its traditionally emotive evocation of *Linos*—marks a further increase in emotive stimulus. The same purpose is achieved by the accumulation of intensive compound epithets, by the strong alliteration and assonance in lines 154–56, and by the personification of Wrath in line 155. The first emotional gestures that are clearly indicated come in lines 202–3 when we are told that the Atreidai wept for grief and struck the ground in anger. All this, together with the cumulative effect of the repeated emotional motifs, would prepare us—unconsciously, perhaps, if we were an audience in a theatre seeing the play for the first time—for the appalling scene that is to come, a scene which, if imposed on us in cold blood, might cause us to feel *stúgos* and *ékplēxis* rather than compassionate grief.

**Lines 205–17** Agamemnon is still in a state of *tarachḗ.* On the one hand, he is affected by *storgḗ* for his daughter, "the delight of his home," and by the horror of "polluting a father's hands with streams from the slaughter of a virgin." On the other, there is the duty of loyalty to the army whose leader he is. His decision to yield to the second motive is expressed in strange terms "because it is right to desire virginal blood with over-angry anger"—or, if *orgḗ* here has its more general meaning of swelling passion, we should translate (with Fraenkel) "with over-passionate passion." Editors for centuries, as Fraenkel observes, have objected to "this intolerable expression" with its tautology and hyperbole. But these, as we have seen, are normal in highly emotional speech, and the violence of the sentiment is psychologically appropriate. Agamemnon's decision is not the result of rationally weighing the arguments for and against the sacrifice. It is an emotional conflict between the *storgé* of a father and the bloodlust of angry warriors (compare ll. 48 and 230) who will strike down whatever stands in the way of their revenge, even an innocent girl. Agamemnon uses the strongest possible term, *thémis* for the truly monstrous assertion that it is right and lawful to passionately desire the blood of a virgin (this word is used twice to emphasize the pity of an unmarried girl's early death). He has to wrench himself away from moral standards as well as from personal affection if he is to commit this appalling deed. That is why he uses such strong language in making his decision. But we must feel a flicker of compassion for him when he adds the pathetically futile prayer, "May it be well" (echoing the earlier refrain).

**Lines 218–27** The Chorus has no doubt about the nature of this decision which is metaphorically identified with a change of wind (so, too, less emphatically in line 187)—a typical Aeschylean blending of actuality and symbolism. Agamemnon, they sing, was now "blowing an impious, impure, unholy wind-change of heart-and-mind" (*phrēn*), and "from then he changed his thinking-and-feeling (*phroneîn*) towards the utterly reckless deed." (Translators tend to emphasize the mental process of decision-making here, but Aeschylus keeps the emotional element in mind by using *phrēn*.) With a touch of *philanthrōpía* the Chorus reflects that his recklessness is a regularly observable phenomenon once a person is overcome by psychological derangement.

**Lines 228–47** This passage brilliantly exemplifies the ability of the Greek lyric poets to paint a heart-rending scene in a brief compass. Though the description of Iphigeneia's death lasts only for twenty lines its emotional impact is as powerful as any scene in Greek tragedy, and in performance it had the advantage over a messenger's description of a catastrophe of being supported by music and dancing. It incorporates several favourite *éleoi*—the death of an innocent marriageable girl (like Polyxena and Macaria), the agony of a parent compelled not only to witness but to cause his child's death (like Medea), and the contrast between present disaster and former happiness.

If line 239—literally "pouring to the ground dyes of saffron"—means "letting fall to the ground her saffron raiment" in the sense of disrobing herself so as to stand naked before what Tennyson in his brilliant reenactment of the scene in *A Dream of Fair Women* calls "the stern, black-bearded kings with wolfish eyes," then we have a startling and unique emotional gesture. Iphigeneia in a last desperate effort to soften the hearts of the angry warlords lets her robe fall to the ground and stands before them totally naked, hoping that the sheer helplessness and innocence of her young body will move them to pity. She cannot speak because her "fair-prowed mouth" has been gagged as Agamemnon ordered. (The second element in the adjective is not "meaningless" as Denniston and Page say: it is there to remind us of the ships that await release.) So she can only "strike each one of the sacrificers with a pity-seeking dart (*oxymoron*) from her eye" and let her whole body speak, "standing out clear to see as in a picture" (l. 242). (One may think, in modern terms, of Botticelli's *Birth of Venus*.) Fraenkel, who supports the view that Iphigeneia disrobes herself (so, too, Thomson and Headlam, Rose, and Groeneboom), compassionately comments, "In the general picture of her appearance, the element of *phíloikton* rises to a level that almost unnerves one." (He contrasts "the simple grandeur" of this scene with the ostentatious care for decorum shown by Polyxena in *Hecuba* lines 558–70.)

If this interpretation is accepted, the order of events would be this: Agamemnon orders the attendants to take his daughter and raise her over the altar like an animal for sacrifice "wrapped in her clothes and drooping forward (as he anticipates) in all her spirit." (The alliteration and word order in line 134 hardly allow one to take *pantì thumôi* as referring to the attendants, though Fraenkel does so.) Agamemnon also orders them first to gag her to prevent possible words of ill omen. But after they have gagged her and before they seize her Iphigeneia slips off her robe and lets her eyes and her body make a last appeal—the appeal of helpless, innocent, beautiful young womanhood. (The scholiast emphasizes the element of beauty in the phrase "as in a picture," rightly, I think, cf. *Hecuba* lines 560–61.) Our last glimpse of Iphigeneia, then, will not be that of an overwhelmed, drooping victim but of a royal princess of the heroic age (like Cassandra) making one last desperate, but not ignoble, bid for her life.

But this order of events and the view that "pouring to the ground dyes of saffron" means disrobing herself have been strongly contested. . . . Undeniably there are strong, but not decisive, arguments against it. (Maas's suggestion that a vase-painting showing Iphigeneia fully clothed during the sacrifice was Aeschylus's model here is only a very remote possibility.)

In *dubia* of this kind, where the arguments are strong on both sides and reputable scholars radically disagree, our best guide may be something similar to the maxim of textual critics in similar circumstances—instead of *difficilior lectio potior, audacior sententia potior.* If we adopt the more daring interpretation—more daring since complete disrobement of this kind is unparalleled in Greek literature, though Polyxena bares her body to the navel and other heroines, as we have seen, bare their breasts in appeals—we can take it as a typically Aeschylean touch of *ékplēxis.* The shock is only momentary and not enough to numb our feelings of pity.

It seems likely that the reference to saffron carries colour symbolism, but its primary relevance is widely disputed. Various suggestions are: a royal colour for a princess; a nuptial colour to suggest the pathos of dying unmarried; a cult colour for Artemis; a festive colour; the colour of blood; the colour of tears. The most likely intention, perhaps, is to sustain the imagery of what Lebeck calls "the endless flow of blood" in the trilogy, anticipating the blood-coloured tapestries on which Agamemnon will walk to his death and the blood-coloured garment that Orestes displays in *Libation-Bearers.*

In lines 242–46 Aeschylus increases the pitifulness by a "flash-back" to the happy days before the declaration of war when Iphigeneia charmed the same ruthless commanders by singing to them "lovingly" after dinners in her "loving" father's palace (*phílos, phílou* and cf. *philoíktōi* in l. 241). All such love is far from her now. The poignant scene, however, is startlingly disrupted by a brutal word describing her virginity, *ataú-rōtos,* "unbulled" (l. 245). Editors for the most part have tried to emasculate this expression. Fraenkel translates it as "virgin" and quotes Wilamowitz's suggestion that it is perhaps a "hieratic" term. Denniston and Page find it "extraordinary and apparently brutal," but renders it as "chaste." Thomson and Headlam say nothing about it, though Thomson translates "pure and spotless." Rose merely compares the metaphor with ll. 1125–26, "Keep the bull from the cow." Groeneboom does not comment on its tone.

The alternative to such palliatives is to accept that Aeschylus intended the term "unbulled" to be brutal and shocking with the full force that it carries in *Lysistrata* line 217. The bull is an obvious symbol of savage and angry male violence, which is exactly what is causing Iphigeneia's death here, though not in a sexual form. (But modern psychologists might regard the shedding of a virgin's blood as a kind of rape.) Such a symbolism would serve to highlight the innocence and gentleness of this scene-within-a-scene of the girl singing "with pure voice" (l. 244) at her father's banquets, in contrast with the scene now as she stands gagged among "the war-loving commanders" (l. 230). The emotional power is strengthened by the *hyperbaton* of the word order in the full phrase— "with pure, being unbulled, utterance, her loving father's fortune-bring-ing (what irony!) paean she lovingly honoured." A similar use of gross sexual symbolism will be suggested on ll. 1442–47, but there Aeschylus's aim is to evoke disgust towards the speaker and not pity for the victim.

**Lines 248–57** With masterly artistic control Aeschylus avoids describ-ing the actual killing. If he had not done so he would have reduced the effect of the two main climaxes of pity that are to come. The Chorus, deeply moved, takes refuge in platitudes.

**Lines 258–81** This is mostly *êthos*, but two emotions are touched on— *phthónos* in a weak sense (l. 263), and joy expressed in terms of hyperbole by Clytemnestra (l. 266) and with glad tears by the Chorus (l. 270). The deferential terms of the Coryphaios's address to the queen and his use of the term *krátos* for her power (cf. ll. 10 and 104 and the character Kratos in *Prometheus*) echo the Watchman's apprehensions. The marked *p* allit-eration in line 268 expresses "breathless excitement" (Fraenkel) at the good news of the capture of Troy. In much of what Clytemnestra says until Agamemnon has been ensnared we must watch out for *allēgoríai*, double-meaning phrases that "speak to those who understand." When in line 266 she speaks of "joy beyond expectation," she probably has her own private joy in mind as well as the joy of victory—the joy of knowing that soon she will have her revenge on Agamemnon (as her *Schadenfreude* in lines 1391–92 suggests).

**Lines 281–316** Clytemnestra's superbly vivid and imaginative speech about the chain of beacons serves two main purposes, one ethical, the other symbolical. In terms of characterization one feels—and can hardly help admiring—the queen's energy leaping and pulsating with the flames that are so joyous (l. 287), vigorous (l. 296), exuberant (l. 301), and vic-tory-bringing (l. 314). Her description embodies what the Watchman told us (l. 11) about her "hopeful heart." (The Greek word *elpís*, as Verrall observed on line 11, can include what we would call imagination.)

Symbolically the already established imagery of torches as emblems of joy becomes prominent here (compare ll. 21ff. and 88ff.). But there is a further possibility. Hephaistos (l. 281) was notorious in mythology for having been cuckolded by his wife Aphrodite when she committed adultery with Ares, as described in *Odyssey* 8.267ff. Artemidoros says that to dream about Hephaistos foretells adultery. Is this then Aeschylus's first *sotto voce* hint at the queen's adulterous relationship with Aigisthos?

**Lines 320–50**  In this equally vivid and imaginative speech on what Clytemnestra imagines is now happening in the captured city we can feel a sense of pity for what both the conquered and the conquerors have been suffering. Then, ominously, she speaks of the risk that lust (*érōs*) for plunder and destruction may cause the destroyers to be destroyed. Even more ominous, in view of Iphigeneia's recently described fate, is her phrase "the wakeful sufferings of the dead." Finally when she says "may the good have the strength to prevail" (the *krátos* motif again) she does not mean what the Chorus meant in their refrain and its echo in line 255: she means may her own plans succeed, so that she may be the victor in the last lap (l. 314). In all these ambiguous remarks of hers we should remember how Demetrios signalized the use of *allēgoría* to evoke fear.

**Lines 355–402**  The Chorus, after a brief, and not very exuberant, expression of thanksgiving—their joy in line 270 has been muted by Clytemnestra's ominous remarks—now turn to reflections on crime and punishment. The symbolism of the net is emphatically introduced with two synonyms (ll. 358, 361), and the image of light (l. 389) is momentarily perverted to something frightening and baleful.

**Lines 404–87**  With the presentation of Helen to our full attention here (contrast line 62) the fourth main emotional theme of the play comes into prominence—*érōs,* with *póthos* and *storgē*. The consequence of Helen's yielding to *érōs* is the pitiful *páthos* of Menelaos and the grieving *storgē* of the Argive citizens for their dead kinsmen in the Troad. Menelaos's yearning for "her that is over the ocean" puts into one word in the Greek (*huperpontías*) all the feeling of the folk-song "My bonny lies over the ocean, My bonny lies over the sea, My bonny lies over the ocean, Oh bring back my bonny to me" (compare *Persians* ll. 135–39). The double power of Helen's beauty is obliquely expressed: its aesthetic appeal is implied in Menelaos's total loss of appreciation of "shapely statues" in his palace (such *anorexia aesthetica* is a characteristic feature of this kind of mental and emotional state), while its erotic power is implied in the phrase used by the "seers of the house" (l. 409)—"man-(or husband-) loving (cf. on line 856) steps (or traces)." Menelaos's utter prostration is vividly expressed (with asyndeton) in the phrase "silence, without honour, without reproach, without belief." The description of Helen's phantom in the house and of her elusive form "slipping through his arms" in dreams, presents an unforgettably pitiful picture in the few lines.

"These," we are told, "are the woes at the hearth within the house." The assonance between the words for "woes" (*ákhē*) and the word for the empty look in Menelaos's eyes (*akhēníais*) links the two ideas together. But, the Chorus continues, there are worse woes in the houses of the citizens of Argos, woes that "touch the very liver" (l. 432)—grief for the dead Greeks at Troy. This is the grief of *storgḗ* not *érōs*. There is also an aesthetic element in this grief, as the poignant quatrain in ll. 452–55 records:

> They, in their shapely beauty,
> Near to the Trojan ramparts
> Keep their graves. But the hostile land
> Covers the men who possessed it.

This is an isometric rendering of the rhythms of this quatrain which consists of two pherecratics and a glyconic and a pherecratic (or two pherecratics and a priapeum), a gentle Aeolic rhythm. The same metrical group has already been used in lines 381–84, 399–402, 416–19, 433–46, and it will appear once more in lines 471–73. It constitutes a rhythmical refrain which isolates and links together the salient themes of the ode— avenging justice, the sin of Paris, the grief of Menelaos, the deaths of Greeks at Troy, their burial far from home, and a prayer to be spared from the cruel victories and defeats of war.

The quatrain quoted from lines 452–55 is also linked verbally with that describing Menelaos's loss of love for beautiful statues by the repetition of the word for "shapely" (*eúmorphos*). As editors have noticed, the grief expressed here for citizens killed in a foreign land may echo the feelings of the Athenians in the time of their costly campaign in Egypt. But it also expresses the sadness of all war graves. One may recall Rupert Brooke's lonely tomb on Scyros or the cemeteries of the soldiers who died opposite Troy in Gallipoli in 1915. Here, in a characteristically Greek way, a wry sense of the irony of fate is inserted into the pathos—the possessors are possessed, the victors are vanquished (as Clytemnestra foresaw in line 340).

**Lines 456–74**   The *phthónos* (l. 456) aroused among the Argive citizens by the deaths of their relatives "through another man's wife" turns to

angry resentment (*kótos*, smouldering anger) in l. 456. Worse still, as the
Chorus's "anxiety" (l. 460) suggests, the gods and the dark Erinyes may
be aroused by all this killing to send "the man who is lucky without
justice" down into darkness. Here as elsewhere several translators, including Fraenkel, assume that the anxiety is mental not visceral. In fact
it is probably both.

**Lines 475–78** The symbolism of fire is given another twist. The
Chorus observe that one can interpret a fire signal wrongly, letting one's
heart flare up like a flame and then sink down when the truth is known.
And—here Aeschylus is devising further variations on the fire theme—
aren't rumours spread by women like brushwood fires, quickly lit and
quickly quenched (if that is how we should take the metaphor in line
485)? The fire imagery lingers on in lines 489–97.

**Lines 503–86** The Herald renews the note of joy, now that his passionate love (*érōs*, l. 540) and *póthos* (l. 545) for his native land are sat-
isfied. His opening speech is full of joyous light-symbolism, the gleam
(*phéngos*) of day (l. 504), the light (*pháos*) of the sun (l. 508), the "sun-
facing" statues of the gods with brightness in their eyes (ll. 519–20), the
glory of a victory "that brings light in the night-time" (l. 522). But a
shadow falls when the Coryphaios talks of "groaning from a darkened
*phrēn*." This the Herald understands—presumably from the Coryphaios's
tone of voice—to imply some feeling of abhorrence or loathing (*stúgos*,
l. 547). Questioned on this, the Coryphaios adopts the precaution prescribed by the Watchman—"silence as a remedy against harm." Asked
then, "How so? Were you afraid of someone in the absence of the rulers?"
he replies "Yes, to the extent that death would have been a boon." Once
again fear has quenched joy.

The Herald returns to the theme of victory and success. He voices
some self-pity and some *philanthrōpía* for the sufferings of the troops at
Troy (with a touch of *stúgos* in ll. 558ff.). But today, he concludes, is a
day of brightness, a day for boasting and exultation, a time to dedicate
bright spoils of armour in the temples of the gods.

**Lines 587–614** Clytemnestra enters on a note of joy—joy at having
been proved right about the meaning of the beacons despite the ridicule
of male chauvinists like the Chorus. Then she turns to a tricky task. She
has to send a message to her husband that will both reassure him and
also prevent the listening Chorus from bursting out with a denial of what

she says. She succeeds in this by skillful use of phrases that can be taken in two ways, as the Coryphaios hints in lines 615–16 (*allēgoría*).

One feature of the queen's speech deserves special attention. In line 605 she uses a distinctly erotic term (see Fraenkel) to describe her husband, "the darling (*erásmion*) of the city." This word, as Fraenkel notices, does not recur in Attic Greek until Plato. Fraenkel describes it as "undignified and almost offensive." But it is a word that a loving wife might use with reference to her husband. Here, however, by adding "of the city," she makes it clear "to those who understand" that he certainly isn't *her* darling. Immediately afterwards, as if she feels that she has implied too much she goes on to assert that she "destroyed no seal in the length of time and knew no delight nor blameful word from another man, any more than dyeings (or dippings) of bronze" (ll. 609–12). The surface meaning of the first phrase is obvious: husbands regularly sealed up their treasuries and storehouses when going abroad, as Fraenkel amply documents. But the Triclinian Ms. has the interlinear gloss "the seal of the conjugal bed." Fraenkel dismisses this as an "absurd explanation," but Thomson and Headlam and Denniston and Page (quoting Herodas l. 55) accept it, without amplification. Nor does Fraenkel say why he thinks it absurd.

In fact the scholiast has good reason for his view. Aeschylus and everyone in his audience who was familiar with the *Odyssey* knew that Aigisthos had seduced Clytemnestra during Agamemnon's absence and had persuaded her to join in his plot to kill the king: see *Odyssey* 3.263–66, 11.421–23, and 24.96–97. (Nothing is said about the murder of Iphigeneia in either epic: on the contrary if she is the Iphianassa named in *Iliad* 9.145, she was still alive in the ninth year of the war.) Consequently the queen's adultery would be in the minds of the poet and his audience. Also, no doubt, in the play itself, the citizens of Argos would also be expected to know about it. (Pindar in *Pythians* 11.22–30, speculating on whether it was *érōs* for Aigisthos or revenge for Iphigeneia that motivated Clytemnestra mentions the gossip of citizens in such a case, and cf. lines 445ff. above.) On the other hand the citizens are unlikely to have had any certain knowledge of the plot to murder the king, though they might guess at it since Aigisthos had every reason to seek revenge. So the dark secret that the Watchman hinted at, and the *stúgos* mentioned in line 547, are more likely to refer to the adulterous union than the intended murder.

The erotic implication of "the seal" is strengthened by Clytemnestra's following denial of "delight . . . from another man," as Denniston and Page notice. Aeschylus in planning the play apparently chose to emphasize the revenge motive for Clytemnestra's crime, but at the same time he sustains what G. M. Hopkins called "underthought" about the sexual motive presented by Homer, until it becomes explicit in lines 1435ff. In *Frogs* lines 1043–44 Aristophanes makes Aeschylus say that, unlike Euripides, he never portrayed a lovesick woman in his plays. This is true so far as we know. But he undoubtedly presents the disastrous effects of *érōs* in the case of Helen and Cassandra. See further on line 1224 and lines 1434ff.

The meaning of "dyeings (or dippings) of bronze" in line 612 is a notorious crux. Whatever it means, the Chorus is likely to have felt a *frisson* of fear from its *allēgoría,* a fear doubtless enhanced by the sheer audacity of the whole speech and by the challenging demeanour of the queen which would amount to saying "I dare you to deny it." Their reply contains an implicit warning for the Herald.

**Lines 617–80** After Clytemnestra has gone back into the palace the emotional tension relaxes again, and our thoughts and feelings are directed away from Argos for a while. There are mild contrasts of gladness and gloom in the Herald's account of what happened (ll. 636–37 and 667–69), with two references to divine anger (*kótos* in the question of the Coryphaios in line 635, *mênis* in the reply, line 649). The abnormal alliance of fire and water (ll. 650–51), and the personification of the storm as "an evil shepherd" (l. 657), and the description of the sea as being "aflower with corpses" (a truly Baudelairean phrase if *antheîn* has full force in line 659), are all images of perverted nature. Light-imagery recurs three times (ll. 658, 668, 676) and darkness once (l. 653). The Herald's hope that the royal houses (of Agamemnon and Menelaos) will be saved from utter destruction by Zeus implies some latent fear.

**Lines 681–749** The Chorus is perturbed by the news of Menelaos's disappearance and by the Herald's somber reference to "the destruction of the race." All this trouble, they assert, is the fault of a woman, Helen, who (as her name implies) brought hell to ships and men and cities, and both kin and care (*kêdos* l. 699) to Troy. In their description of her light-hearted departure from Sparta the mood of voluptuous sensuality is strong, as we learn how she came out from the luxuriously woven curtains of her bedroom (or bed) and sailed away to Troy on the breeze of Zephyros (who according to one account was the father of Eros). The amorous ambiance is supported by the rhythm that breaks at lines 691–95 into *anacreontics,* the metre named after the poet of love and pleasure who lived in Athens when Aeschylus was a boy.

The romantic mood changes very quickly when "many-manned hunters" (the epithet used of Helen in a very different sense in line 62) follow on her track. Strife, Eris, takes over from Eros in line 698—Strife who, as the audience would remember, initiated the chain of events that led to the Trojan war when she hurled the golden apple inscribed "For the fairest" among the goddesses on Olympus.

In lines 706–16 we have a brief movement from festive joy to grief and lamentation. The much discussed parable of the lion cub emblemizes a similar development from *cháris* and *philía* to savagery and destruction, as this charming welcome guest (like Paris and Helen at first) becomes an avenging sacrificer—"and the house was bespattered with blood." There is a brief lull in ll. 739–49 (aptly expressed in iambics after trochees as Lloyd-Jones notes). In the description of Helen as that "heart-stinging flower of *érōs* with a tender weapon (*oxymoron*) in her eyes" perhaps Aeschylus wishes us to remember "the pitiful weapon" of the eyes of Iphigeneia in 241–42. Denniston and Page argue that the lion cub is not simply a symbol of Helen but of all the circumstances leading to the sack of Troy (compare Lloyd-Jones). In fact it probably symbolizes both ideas under the general notion of love and loveliness turning to savagery and destruction. A further variation on the theme of light-and-darkness is added in the complex antithesis between a house dark with smoke but bright with Justice and a palace bright with gold but dark with crime, a piece of chiaroscuro worthy of Rembrandt.

**Lines 257–781**    Recapitulation. We have been through many alternations of emotions in this part of the play—joy at the victory, anxiety at Clytemnestra's veiled threats and challenges, pity for the sufferings of both the Greeks and the Trojans, compassion for the *póthos* of Menelaos and for the grief of those who mourn dead kinsmen at Troy (and possibly sympathy for their anti-war resentment), scorn, perhaps, for the Chorus's stupid anti-feminism, anxiety again when the Herald and Chorus talk of dispirited gloom and a death wish, a touch of *stúgos* at Clytemnestra's defiant lies, remote sympathy for the sufferings of the Greeks in the storm described by the Herald, and a bittersweet response to the glowing picture of that lethal and beautiful femme fatale, Helen. In the last three stanzas the prevailing mood is apprehension about what may happen to people at the height of their prosperity, such as (it is implied) victorious Agamemnon. (Compare ll. 338–47.)

**Lines 782–809**    The Chorus anxiously does its best to warn Agamemnon against treachery and hypocrisy, but fails.

**Lines 810–913** In this crucial confrontation between the king (with his concubine Cassandra) and the queen, considerations of characterisation and plot are dominant. But one question of *êthos* must be answered before the degree of our pity, fear, hate and repulsion, towards both characters can be determined. Attitudes towards Agamemnon vary between Fraenkel's whole-hearted admiration and Denniston and Page's sharp fault-finding. Three points need to be kept in mind. First, the Watchman and the Chorus plainly like him. Secondly, in his words to the Chorus and the queen he shows, as I see it, insensitivity and arrogance and—worse still to the Greek mind—stupidity. (Editors have missed a hint here: when he praises Odysseus as his only faithful and trustworthy friend at Troy the Athenian audience may well have thought "Poor deluded man, to trust such a notorious deceiver." The remark is meant, I believe, to show that Agamemnon just doesn't understand "the mirror of society," as he claims in line 839. His subsequent deception by his wife, despite the Chorus's warnings, will prove this only too clearly.) Thirdly, to my mind there is a distinct touch of gloating, *epichairekakía,* in his description of the fate of Troy, especially in his remark about the "fatty breaths of wealth"—note the expressive *p*-alliteration in the Greek—that rise from the burning city. (Older Athenians would remember the burning of Athens by the Persians twenty-two years earlier.) The same *Schadenfreude* is implied when he boasts that "the fierce beast of Argos . . . the ravening lion licked his fill of princely blood" (ll. 827–28). The contrast between that kind of language and Clytemnestra's sympathetic descriptions of the sorrows of the Trojans (ll. 320ff.) is not in his favour. (Incidentally the only time that Agamemnon mentions Clytemnestra in the *Iliad* is when he says he prefers his concubine Chryseis to her, in book 1.) In fact apart from the problematical degree of his moral culpability in sacrificing Iphigeneia he satisfies Aristotle's prescription for the best kind of tragic hero—a reasonably decent man with fatal flaws of judgment and character, though we may well feel that his punishment was excessive. If Agamemnon were such a model of kingly rectitude as Fraenkel believes, his death would have been foul and repulsive (*miarós*) in Aristotle's view (*Poetics*).

As to Clytemnestra, we have seen and heard enough of her to know how formidable and yet how warmly imaginative she is. In *Odyssey* 3.265–72, Nestor says that "she was endowed with goodness of heart-and-mind (*phresí*)" until Aigisthos "led her, in mutual willingness, to his home." Aeschylus, I think, intends to give an impression of perverted goodness rather than of innate villainy.

Agamemnon's opening speech is coldly unemotional apart from the touches of *Schadenfreude* already noticed, and has a passing, but significant reference to *phthónos* in line 833. In contrast, Clytemnestra's reply palpitates with warm, but hypocritical emotion and with extraordinarily rich imagery. She addresses the Chorus first with a kind of warning challenge—"I shall not be ashamed to tell my husband-loving (or "man-loving") ways to you" (ll. 856–57)—"And," the implication is, "I dare you to deny them." By using the ambiguous term *philánoras* she implies to the Chorus (who used the same term in connection with Helen in line 411) "You know that this means Aigisthos to me, but Agamemnon doesn't." Fraenkel rejects the possibility of an intended double meaning here and warns readers against "any concession to the playful ingenuity shown by Headlam, among others." But gibes are not arguments, and readers less prejudiced against the notion that Aeschylus would not wish to remind his audience of Clytemnestra's notorious adultery may prefer the views of Headlam on this.

Thomson and Headlam also find erotic innuendoes—and rightly I believe—in two other phrases used by Clytemnestra in this speech. The first is "bewailing the lamp-holdings even untended" (l. 891). The primary reference is probably to the beacons (see Fraenkel). But as Thomson and Headlam fully establish, the lamp is frequently mentioned in Greek poetry as a companion of erotic scenes (and cf. Artemidoros 67.14–15). Secondly, as Thomson and Headlam also notice, "the time that slept with me" (l. 894) suggests a very different kind of bedfellow. As I see it, such *allēgoríai* are Aeschylus's method of keeping the audience aware of the *stúgos* inside the palace, until it is blatantly revealed by Clytemnestra in lines 1431ff. At the end of her speech, as she orders the servants to spread the blood-coloured tapestries for Agamemnon to tread on, she uses another kind of double entendre, "that Justice may bring him to an *unexpected* house-and-home," cf. Agamemnon's bitter remark about how he had hoped to be treated on his return home in *Odyssey* 11.430–32.

When Agamemnon, wary, as he is, of divine as well as human *phthónos,* demurs at such an act of wanton pride and self-glorification as trampling on precious fabrics, Clytemnestra with brilliant dialectic first quells his religious scruples and then overcomes his *aidōs* towards popular reproach by the clever aphorism "The man who incurs no envy (in the bad sense, *phthónos*) is not enviable" (in the good sense). Her final argument is a subtle feminine one, "You'll prove your power (*krátos* again) by willingly yielding to me on this"—a pretty phrase from a woman whose masculine power we have known since the Watchman's description of her in line 11.

**Lines 931–57** The tense and crucial thirteen lines of stichomythia in lines 931–44, a verbal duel for life or death, must have given the Athenian audience the kind of excitement that Romans would feel when a gladiator wielding the sword and shield of a warrior fought a wily *retiarius* with his entangling net and trident. Our pity and fear for Agamemnon when he yields must be tempered with recognition of his insensitive weakness and his folly in thinking that he can escape *phthónos* by having his shoes removed before he tramples on the tapestries and by a prayer. And how can one defend a man (from himself) who admits that he feels a great deal of *aidōs* in destroying costly tapestries by walking on them, and then goes and does it? Clytemnestra defiantly rejected shame in line 856. Agamemnon claims to feel *aidōs,* but acts as if he had none.

Finally Agamemnon, with characteristic coldness towards the feelings of others, orders Clytemnestra to bring "this stranger here graciously (or 'kindly') into the house" adding pious platitudes about heaven's favour towards the gentle use of *krátos* and about the unpleasantness of being a slave. "Besides," he adds, "she has come with me as the army's choice gift, a flower chosen out of many things of value." After this suggestion that valuable things should be handled with care he proceeds to trample on the precious tapestries. Fraenkel finds pity in Agamemnon's introduction of Cassandra. Perhaps he is right, but I find his words frigid, insensitive, hypocritical (how gently did Agamemnon use his *krátos* at Troy?) and egotistic. And how does Princess Cassandra like being described as a slave (cf. Clytemnestra's bitter variation on the same theme in lines 1035–45 and 1065–68)? And how does Clytemnestra like being ordered to be kind to her husband's concubine? In fact the queen totally ignores Agamemnon's command and leaves Cassandra standing outside the palace.

Fraenkel seems to be uncharacteristically off-balance in his treatment of this scene, perhaps because of his determination to defend Agamemnon. He scornfully rejects the view that the king has "any other feeling for his captive beyond that of pity for her fate," meaning, I take it, that no *érōs* is involved. But Clytemnestra had no illusions about that (see on ll. 1434ff. and cf. *Trojan Women* ll. 252–55 and *Hecuba* l. 829). Secondly, Fraenkel takes the view that Cassandra is not recognizable in this scene. Apart from Wilamowitz's suggestion that Cassandra's prophetic costume (compare ll. 1264–65) would make it clear that she was the famous prophetic princess of Troy, would anyone but the grossest ignoramus in the audience have failed to guess on the basis of the epic tradition, who this female companion of the king was? Aeschylus keeps her very much in the background so as not to distract attention from the main action. But her silent presence adds strongly to the emotional tension of this and the following scene.

The symbolism of the king's last words (apart from his deathcry) "I go into the halls of the house trampling on crimson" and of his corresponding action has been fully explored elsewhere. But it is strange, in view of recent studies on the colours and colour-sense of the Greeks, that *porphúras* is still sometimes translated "purple" here. The meanings of the word seem to have extended from brown to crimson, and here, of course, the colour will be that of blood.

**Lines 958–74** The suspense becomes almost unbearable while Agamemnon moves towards the House of Death. It is shared by the Chorus (who are anxious) and by Clytemnestra (who is hopeful) about the king's fate—and we in the audience must wonder, too, whether perhaps he will draw back, even though we know from the tradition that he is doomed to die. (If the acting and the language are compelling enough an audience may forget its foreknowledge and live by empathy in the present moment of the play.)

Clytemnestra's speech during Agamemnon's progress has been much criticized. Denniston and Page, for example, find "an unsatisfactory muddle" in line 961, while line 965 is "most abnormal" and the syntax of lines 966ff. is "pitiable" and whatever the true reading may be there "the sentence as a whole is inelegant enough." Denniston and Page also note "indifference to repetition" in the use of various words for "house" in lines 961, 962, 964, 966, 968, 971, 972. But if we are to appreciate the dramatic and emotional power of the finale of this tremendous scene we should, perhaps, feel more pity for the persons concerned than for the syntax, and recognize that abnormal situations may provoke abnormal language. Here is a woman who has long been waiting and planning for this very climax. As Agamemnon advances towards the fatal door she fears that at any moment he may sense danger and withdraw (like Cassandra in lines 1306–11 and 1323), or else the Chorus may dare to shout "Don't go in" (compare ll. 1331–34).

As to the remarkable repetitions of references to the House of Death, if we accept the suggestion mentioned on lines 35–37 that the house, whose facade forms the permanent background to the whole play, has the force of a silent character throughout, then we may take it that Aeschylus here intends to intensify our awareness of its sinister menace. A modern stage manager would effect this by projecting a lurid spotlight on it.

Deprived of such mechanical aids Aeschylus has to use words, though he has also already employed one simple but ingenious visual aid, the red fabrics that point to the fatal door. This is the first scene in which the house plays an obtrusive part as a thing to promote terror. But Aeschylus has been consistently leading up to this by no less than twenty-six previous references to the house—first the five already noticed in the Watchman's speech, and then twenty-one spaced over the intervening scenes (ll. 155, 157, 208, 244, 310, 343, 409, 415, 427, 518, 579, 606, 679, 851, 862, 865, 867, 897, 911, 914, 948). This frequency can be partly explained by the fact that the genre of this play is a homecoming, a macabre *nóstos*. But it is partly, I believe, a means of highlighting the abominable house with its pitiful and fearful deeds in the past, present, and future. The house will again be thrown into ghastly prominence in lines 1306ff. (Eugene O'Neill makes a similarly effective use of the Mannion's home in his modern version of the *Oresteia, Mourning Becomes Electra,* and compare Poe's "Fall of the House of Usher.")

The primary function of this extraordinary speech of Clytemnestra is to hold the attention of Agamemnon by talking, talking, talking, for fear that a moment of silence would let him change his mind. Some of the effusive symbolism has sinister undertones. "Ever-renewed ooze of crimson . . . for the dyeing of garments" recalls the saffron-dyed robes of Iphigeneia and "the dyeing of bronze" (compare on l. 239). The word for "of garments" here (*heimátōn*), repeated in line 963, is phonetically close to *haimátōn,* meaning "of blood-flows." Thomson and Headlam suggest that "wine from the unripe grape" (l. 970) refers to the shedding of Iphigeneia's blood, since *ómphax* is used elsewhere to mean "a young virgin." Fraenkel dismisses this as "an unwarranted psychological nicety." But what is more likely to be in the queen's mind here than the first reason for her revenge? In general, the basic pattern of the imagery here—root-leaf-grape, coolness-heat-cold, summer-winter-autumn—resembles the free associations of a patient undergoing psychological analysis. It is true that the total effect is incoherent. But such language and thought is apt for moments of high emotional tension. Bernard Shaw in the *Saturday Review* for March 20, 1897, observed on Cleopatra's outburst at the death of Antony in *Antony and Cleopatra,* beginning

> Oh withered is the garland of the war,
> The soldier's pole is fallen.

"This is not good sense—not even good grammar. If you ask what does it all mean, the reply must be that it means just what its utterer feels. The chaos of its thought is a reflection of her mind."

**Lines 975–1034**   Here we have the most effective expression of *tarachḗ* and of anxious, ill-defined fear in Greek tragedy. Visual imagery—dread is seen as "fluttering" like a distressed bird in front of their hearts— merges into aural imagery—an unwanted, boding song—and merges back again into the visual image of baffling dreams. Then the Chorus sings of the cause of their mental and emotional distress: their *phrḗn* should be confident and hopeful now that victory has been won and the king is home again, but their *thumós* "from inside" keeps chanting "a dirge of the Erinyes." The use of *thumós,* "passion," here (as in the very similar *Persians* lines 10–11) is noteworthy. It is the irrational hard-to-control, dynamic element in the *psuchḗ.* The Chorus finds it irrepressible here. In fact, they go on to sing, one must believe what one's entrails (*splánchna*) "sing" at a time like this, and one must heed what is predicted by "the heart as it whirls in eddies that bring fulfilment against the justified mind"—a strange maelstrom of meaning indeed! But such language is what one would expect in cases of extreme *tarachḗ.* The dominant image of a whirling vortex symbolizes this mental and emotional condition more powerfully than the commoner image of a *storm* at sea. The rhythms of these two stanzas, short, catelectic trochaic dimeters—broken by a swift run of dactyls in the fifth lines—have been compared to the beat of a palpitating heart. The dactyls have another significance: they are apt for prophetic utterances (compare on ll. 104ff.).

In the desperately corrupt third stanza the mind gains control of the "entrails" for a while in some pious philosophizing. But in the fourth stanza the thought of "a man's blood falling to the earth in death" soon sets their *tarachḗ* fluttering again in another highly controversial passage which I paraphrase as: "It was Moira (whose function is to see that everything keeps to its own appointed sphere) who prevented Asklepios from successfully trespassing on Death's territory by restoring a man to life (ll. 1022–24): the same goddess prevents my heart from usurping the province of my tongue by telling me in plain words what it is trying to say. Consequently my heart can only murmur in darkness, with agonizing *thumós,* and without any hope of spinning off a timely thread (of rational discourse), while my *phrḗn* is all ablaze." The "timely thread" means some intelligible word-and-thought (*lógos*) spun from the turbulent heart in the same way as a continuous thread is spun from a tangled mass of wool. (Aeschylus himself is accused of using "concepts like tangled

wool" in "Longinus" 15.5, and of talking "like a holm-oak on fire" in
*Frogs* line 859.) The "conflagration" of the heart-and-mind is a striking
variation of the recurrent flame of fire motif, combining the notions of
heart and force. In simplest terms the passage expresses a commonplace
of poetry ancient and modern—the impossibility of expressing the deepest emotions in lucid words. Whether or not Aeschylus is on the verge of
realizing the existence of the unconscious here I leave to psychologists to
decide.

**Lines 1035–71**   Instead of letting Agamemnon's death cry ring out at
once, or else introducing an agitated messenger to announce his death,
as we might have expected, Aeschylus stretches suspense here and in the
following scene almost to the breaking point. The futile effort of the
queen to lure Cassandra into the palace—"Will you walk into my parlour,
said the Spider to the Fly?"—is ethical rather than emotional, though the
queen makes a passing reference to divine *mênis* in line 1036 and then
flares up angrily herself. Next, Aeschylus modulates from the key of fear
and anger to the key of pity in the remark of the Coryphaios that Cassandra is like a newly caught animal (a comparison which Clytemnestra
distorts into that of a senseless unbroken-in horse straining with bleeding
mouth at the bit) to a direct statement, after the queen has gone, "I pity
her and will not be angry." Pity dominates now.

It is not clear why Aeschylus allowed Clytemnestra to be morally
defeated by Cassandra in this brief interlude. The best explanation, perhaps, is that the scene gives stature to Cassandra and at the same time
emphasizes her tense stillness just before her appalling shrieks in lines
1072ff.

**Lines 1072–1135**   The germ of the heart-rending scene that follows was
perhaps what the ghost of Agamemnon said in Hades in describing his
own death (*Odyssey* 11.421), "I heard the most pitiful (*oiktrotátēn*) cry of
Priam's daughter Cassandra, whom deceitful Clytemnestra killed beside
me." Aeschylus has expanded this into an amazingly effective episode—
the second wave in his *trikumía* of pitiful deaths. At first Cassandra's
agony of terror and grief can only be screamed out in repeated excla-
matory cries and invocations of Apollo. Articulate speech then evolves
by way of a *nomen omen* in which Apollo's name is seen to incorporate a
verb meaning to destroy in Greek (like Apollyon in *The Pilgrim's Progress*). Her next object of conscious recognition is the House of Death,

which she describes in terms reminiscent of the phrase in *Odyssey* 11.420, "The whole floor steamed with blood." She is reacting at first to the abominable crime of Atreus in feasting Thyestes with his children's flesh. Clairvoyantly she can hear the babies bewailing their fate. Immediately afterwards she sees the imminent horror of the death of Agamemnon entangled in "the net." This is described in quick-flash, impressionistic "shots"—the brightness of the victim's body after the bath, "hand reaching out from hand" (like a fisherman's when he draws in a net), and, marked by screams of *é, é, papaî*, the "net of Death." The Chorus represented by the Coryphaios, have been replying up to this in calm iambic trimeters to the irregular lyric metres (partly *dochmiac*) of Cassandra—in a matter-of-fact detached way like elderly uncles dealing with a hysterical niece. The change to dochmiacs in l. 1121 shows that they have begun to react physically to her fearful utterances. They feel their "saffron" blood running back to their hearts as if they had been fatally wounded by a spear.

With two gasps of horror—the sharply accented *á á* seems the best reading here. . .—Cassandra sees the murder of Agamemnon taking place. It is so real to her that she cries out for someone to stop it: "Keep the bull from the cow." The metaphor may have sexual undertones as in line 245, but if so they are fainter here. The following phrase "She has caught him with the black contrivance of the horned one" (Fraenkel) or (preferably, I think) "with the black-horned device" is obscure—a nightmarishly vague and terrifying image like "that two-handed engine at the door" in Milton's *Lycidas*. The Coryphaios and Chorus respond in an iambic trimeter followed by dochmiacs as in ll. 1119–24—an alternation of cool reasoning and excited emotionalism as before.

**Lines 1136–77** Cassandra now changes from horrified clairvoyance about the king's death to self-pity and pity for her kinsfolk. The Chorus, now completely emotional, as the metre shows, compares her—conventionally—to that traditional emblem of sad, but melodious lamentation, the nightingale, who with piteous *phrénes* bewails Itys her son, eaten, like Thyestes' children, by his father. Pathetically Cassandra rejects the comparison as inept (the analytical Greek mind operates even at a moment of high emotion), since the nightingale lives on in a life of sweet melody while she is doomed to "cleaving asunder by the two-edged weapon." (Her voice as she prophesies this has "an ill-boding clang," like that of Calchas in lines 156 and 201.) In 1566ff. her self-pity turns to pitiful lamentation for the fate of Priam and Troy. The Chorus finds her prediction of her own death "shattering to hear," and feels helplessly uncertain about the outcome.

Meanwhile, as the rhythm slows, Cassandra has been gradually growing calmer in iambic trimeters in lines 1148–49, 1160–61, and 1171–72, while the Chorus grows more excited.

**Lines 1178ff.** Now, in regular iambic trimeters, Cassandra discards emotional rhythms and images and turns to rational statement for a while. But a new feeling is expressed in line 1192, *stúgos,* disgust—expressed by *spitting*—for the crimes of Atreus and Thyestes. (Artemis felt the same way about "the feast of the eagles" in line 137.) This prepares the way for the third, and most emphatic expression of loathing in 1228ff. Next *érōs* reappears, here in the form of the vengeful passion of Apollo. The pangs of prophecy seize Cassandra again in line 1214, as her screams indicate, whirling her (compare l. 907) in *taraché* for a moment before she sees the ghastliest vision of all, the children of Thyestes surrealistically holding the intestines and entrails that their own father ate, "a pitiful burden to bear." The first overt reference to Aigisthos in the play follows immediately. He, as a Pelopid, is entitled to the family emblem of the lion, but the symbol is perverted by an *oxymoron* in Cassandra's phase "a weakling lion." (Cf. Shakespeare, *Troilus and Cressida* 3.2: "They that have the voice of lions and the act of hares, are they not monsters?") She adds a frankly sexual description of him as "wallowing in the bed," and then (l. 1228) she turns to describe the queen as a "lewd hound" (*misétēs*). Then Cassandra evokes a menagerie of evil and hateful animals and monsters to express how she loathes her.

The Coryphaios says that he shuddered and felt fear at the description of the fate of the children of Thyestes but is at a loss about the reference to future events (Aeschylus presumably intends the obtuseness of these Argive Elders to increase our sympathy for Cassandra.) So she bluntly tells them that Agamemnon is doomed. The Coryphaios repudiates this notion and adds a conventional gibe about the obscurity of oracles. This incredulity reminds Cassandra of the curse of Apollo and she breaks into screams of agony again. She goes on to repeat her prediction of her own death at the hand of "the two-footed lioness lying with the wolf in the absence of the truly noble lion" (again the sexual reference in this monstrous mating of different beasts). In anger at the gift of prophecy that betrayed her she throws off the symbols of her prophetic vocation, denounces Apollo, predicts the revenge that Orestes will exact, and turns to address the door of the House as "gates of Hades," adding a prayer that at least the stroke that kills her may be immediately mortal. (Compare the similarly cautious prayer of the Chorus in lines 1448–51.)

Here (ll. 1295–96) the Coryphaios pityingly addresses the prophetess as "a woman of much misfortune and of much wisdom as well," but adds "that was a long speech" (like Agamemnon to Clytemnestra in line 916)—more of the blatant male chauvinism in this play (but Fraenkel doesn't think so). A brief, tense argument in stichomythia is broken up when Cassandra shrinks back as she approaches the door. The Coryphaios thinks she is frightened, but it is more disgust than fear as shown by her exclamations, *pheû, pheû* and by the Coryphaios's subsequent word *stúgos*. What has disgusted her, she explains, is "the reek from the house as from a tomb."

Courageously, however, Cassandra goes forward towards the evil door, with what sounds like her last words—"Enough of life" (l. 1314). Then Aeschylus produces a masterstroke of *éleos*. Momentarily her courage fails her. For the first time she begins an appeal for help—she is only a young woman now, another Iphigeneia, not a god-possessed prophetess. She calls to the Chorus "Oh, oh, *xénoi*" and then breaks off in *aposiopesis*. The meaning of that untranslatable word *xénos* here (already used unemphatically by Cassandra in line 1299) is certainly not just "strangers" which in English primarily suggests alienation. On the contrary the word appeals to that basic rule of Greek ethics, *philoxenía* the duty of kindness to "the stranger within the gates." Her appeal, then, is almost as strong as a Christian's appeal "For Christ's sake." But she stops herself—"No indeed (*oútoi:* many editors ignore the force of the emphatic particle), I am not going to raise a frightened cry like a bird at a bush where danger lurks."

After this stifled appeal for help Cassandra steels her heart by thinking of revenge. The Coryphaios, ignoring her formal request to the Chorus to act as witnesses when the day of retributive justice comes, offers his last tribute of compassion—"O woman of much suffering, I pity you for your god-predicted fate!" Cassandra reiterates her desire for revenge. There she might have said her last words. But with a further masterly touch Aeschylus makes her rise above her personal feelings in last words whose tone contrasts sharply with the passionate shrieks, denunciations, and imprecations, of her earlier utterances:

> Alas for mortal doings. When they're prosperous
> One may compare them to a shadow. If they fare ill,

> A touch of a wet sponge wipes their picture out—
> And this I pity more than the other fate.

It is supremely moving that in her last moment Cassandra transcends all self-regarding feelings in compassionate *philanthrōpía* and *Weltschmerz*. Fraenkel comments: "The resigned wisdom of Cassandra's last words is perhaps more deeply moving than all her ecstacies," but this is to over-emphasize the intellectual aspect. What Aeschylus emphasizes is not her wisdom, but the fact that she shows such pity for others when she is in such pitiable misfortune herself.

**Lines 1331–42**   When Cassandra has gone into the House of Death—with her head high, one may guess, as befits a princess—the Chorus, taking up her remark about prosperity and disaster, link it with a symbolical house of disastrous prosperity where no one warns "Don't enter." (Here Aeschylus's usual symbolical progression is reversed: the actual entry into a house comes before the metaphorical event—and perhaps the phrase "Don't enter" reflects what the Chorus feels it should have said to both Agamemnon and Cassandra.) Then, though still not quite convinced about the king's death, they moralize briefly about its "lesson." The metre, regular anapests, reflects their rather surprisingly unexcited mood. Perhaps they march around slowly and meditatively to its rhythm. Presumably Aeschylus is aiming at a moment of *calm* before the storm breaks.

**Lines 1343–71**   The king's two terrible deathcries ring out. They are the first deathcries in extant Greek tragedy, and the most resonant of all. We who encounter them first in cold print must make a great effort of imagination to realize what they would have sounded like when uttered with all the emotional power of a dedicated actor's voice in the Theatre of Dionysos. When they come from inside the dark door, it is almost as if, in the Watchman's words, the House had been given a voice. The Chorus is slow to react emotionally, though the introduction for a moment of catalectic trochaic tetrameters (ll. 1344, 1346–47) indicates their perturbation. Cautious old men that they are, they deliberate on what should be done, some diffidently, others boldly, others uncertainly. There is not a single expression of emotion in the whole debate. The *ékplēxis* of the king's cries has numbed their feelings but not their minds though some degree of *tarachḗ* prevails (compare ll. 1358–61).

**Lines 1372–98** Into this state of perplexity Clytemnestra's defiant appearance standing over the corpses of her victims comes like a blaze of lurid light through darkness. No indecision, no uncertainty, here, only terse realism. The image of the net is now actualized in her gloating description of how she entangled the king in "an evil wealth of dress" (oxymoron). She says all of this in the present tense and presumably with expressive gestures. But the most atrocious part (*stúgos*) of her speech comes when she says, "As he belches forth his life where he lay, spurting out a thin jet of blood, he strikes me with a dark shower of gory dew, and I rejoice no less than the sown fields rejoice at the god-given brightness (of the dew) when the birth-pangs of the ear are at hand." Here is perverted nature imagery at its height. The pure life-giving dew from heaven has become blood pouring from a murdered husband: the joy of the cornfields when their grain comes to the birth has become the fiendish *epichairekakía* of a vengeful wife. Emblems of fruitfulness are turned into symptoms of death.

If the word translated "belches" above (*orugánei*) is authentic, it is a *hapax* in Greek tragedy. As Fraenkel remarks "the coarseness of expression fits in with Clytemnestra's ferocity" (see on lines 1435ff. below). But the emendation is far from being certain.

**Lines 1399–1430** The Coryphaios, speaking in unemotional iambic trimeters, expresses at first only astonishment (which is a mild form of *ékplēxis*) at the queen's brutal and defiant words. When she replies with unmitigated boldness, the whole Chorus reacts more emotionally, mainly in *dochmiacs*. They threaten her with punishment and the hatred of the people (*némesis*). Metrically from ll. 1407–61 we have the reverse of the Cassandra scene, the Chorus chanting in lyric metres, the queen replying calmly in iambic trimeters. She defends herself as in a court of law— Agamemnon murdered her daughter; is she not justified in her retaliation? The Chorus replies that she must be mad and she must die.

**Lines 1431–37** Clytemnestra, weakening a little in her self-reliance, asserts, "Expectancy (*elpís*) does not tread for me in the hall of Fear while Aigisthos kindles fire on my hearth (*hestía*) remaining loyal to me." The metaphor is generally taken as meaning "while Aigisthos continues to be the legitimate lord of the house" with reference to family sacrifices at the hearthstone. That may be so. But "lighting the fire" is not the same as performing a sacrifice, so, in view of the undeniable sexual implications of the succeeding lines, a different meaning may be intended here. (As we have seen, Cassandra has already spoken, in line 1224, of Aigisthos as "wallowing in the bed," and she has called the queen "lewd" in line 1228.) The two words for "heart" in Greek, *hestía* and *eschára,* definitely had sexual meanings. Artemidoros states that to dream of someone kindling fire on a *hestía* means the begetting of children "for at that time a woman grows hotter." On the other hand *hestía* in lines 427, 968, and 1056, is less likely to have any such overtones since the context does not suggest eroticism. Here it is the mention of Aigisthos that suggests sexual implications in the queen's imagery.

Clytemnestra's language becomes overtly erotic in ll. 1493ff. as Fraenkel admits. She describes Agamemnon as "the soothing thing (*meíligma,* used in *Odyssey* 10.217 of bits thrown to dogs) of the Chryseids (contemptuous plural) at Troy." Then, with no justification—Cassandra had no choice, poor girl—she lashes out at Cassandra's reputation calling her, in a unique phrase "mast-rubber" (*histotríbēs*).

Several editors have assumed a sexual *kakémphaton* here, but they have generally, like Fraenkel, held that the less said about that the better: Lloyd-Jones, Denniston and Page, and Rose find the reference to a mast unintelligible. But the fact is that the terms "mast" and "rubbing" have clear and obvious erotic implications elsewhere in Greek literature.

As I see it, then, Aeschylus has deliberately used an obscene term to express the strength of Clytemnestra's other motive for killing the king, namely, sexual hate resulting from his adultery with Chryseis and Cassandra (who asserts the same motive in line 1263). Even though the queen is an adulteress herself now—Homer implies in *Odyssey* 3.265–66 that her seduction by Aigisthos took time—she is infuriated by the fact that Agamemnon has shamed her by bringing Cassandra home as a concubine. (Compare Hermione's jealousy of Andromache in *Andromache.*) The dramatic function of the term, like that of *ataúrotos* in line 244 is presumably to cause a mild *ékplēxis,* as well as to accentuate our *stúgos* for Clytemnestra and our pity for Cassandra.

The sexual imagery continues in lines 1446–47, though here, too, many editors are reluctant to admit it—"There she lies, his lover, and she has brought me a relish (or side-dish, an extra titbit, *paropsónēma*) of my bed (*eunês*), of my luxury (*khlidês*)." Fraenkel rejects *eunês* as corrupt on the grounds that "it is difficult to imagine Clytemnestra speaking of the joys of her bed in a tone such as Hamlet uses to his mother" (why?) and because Clytemnestra's *khlidé* is confined to what she says in lines 1391–92 (again why?). He adds "the lust which wholly possesses the soul of this daemonic woman at the great climax of her life is not sexual, but lust for revenge." This assertion ignores what Homer said about the queen (cf. on ll. 503–86), and what Pindar says about "the nightly couchings that led her astray when she was being tamed in a different bed" (*Pythians* 11.24–25), and what Euripides makes her say in *Electra* lines 1030ff. where she alleges that the bringing home of Cassandra, not the killing of Iphigeneia, caused her to kill her husband.

Thomson and Headlam, Denniston and Page, Groeneboom, Lloyd-Jones, and Rose accept a sexual implication in *paropsónēma* and cite parallels, though not from tragedy. If this view is correct the queen's gibe shows a mixture of hate, jealousy and *epichairekakía* which, as soon appears, arouses sheer revulsion in the Chorus and in the audience.

On the other hand the passing reference to Cassandra's "swan song" (ll. 1444–45) is hardly in keeping with the mocking tone of the rest of the speech. It sounds like the voice of the poet himself introducing what Fraenkel calls "a soft and moving echo" of Cassandra's voice in the previous scene. T. S. Eliot in *Poetry and Drama* discusses a similar emergence of the poet's voice in *Hamlet* when Horatio says

> So have I heard and do in part believe . . .
> But, look, the morn, in russet mantle clad,
> Walks o'er the dew of yon high eastern hill
> Break we our watch up.

Eliot suggests that here is "a kind of musical design which reinforces and is one with the dramatic movement" and which "has checked and accelerated the pulse of our emotion without knowing it," and so "we are lifted for a moment beyond character." The effect is, I think, similar on Clytemnestra's lips. The swan image is part of the last reference to Cassandra in the play, and the poet may feel that he cannot let it be entirely at the mercy of her bitter and malevolent murderer.

**Lines 1448–61** Filled with disgust that their queen should use such language and reveal such ugly feelings, the Chorus (with the same exclamation of loathing, *pheû,* that Cassandra used in line 1307) wishes for death and then with typical anti-feminist prejudices they find it particularly distressing that their "kindest protector" should have died at a woman's hand. They go on to sing of Helen's madness, an *érōs* that turned to *éris* (compare l. 698).

**Lines 1462–1512** Significant rhythm: Clytemnestra now begins to argue with the Chorus (until line 1576) in anapests (which the Chorus

began to use in line 1455). Presumably this congruence of rhythms indicates that she is beginning to feel sympathy for the despair and grief
of the Argive elders, while, in turn, their emotions are becoming less
violent. The queen's words correspond to the implications of this change
of rhythm. She is no longer brutally vindictive. She deprecates the
Chorus's death wish and defends Helen from their rancour (*kótos*). In
reply the Chorus turns its minds away from her and—almost like Cassandra—visualize the daemon of the accused House, "settling like a hateful raven" on the body of the king. (As already noted, to dream of a
raven, according to Artemidoros indicates an adulterer.) Clytemnestra
seizes on this line of defence—"That's right: the thrice-glutted daemon
of the race is to blame." The Chorus agrees, "Yes, it is the embodiment
of wrath *ménis*." Then they give expression to the wave of compassionate
grief that sweeps over them at last, by singing the moving refrain that
has been analysed [elsewhere]. It contains a potent symbol of revulsion
and fear towards Clytemnestra in the phrase, "There you lie in this web
of a spider." If Aeschylus and his audience knew that some female spiders
kill their mates the symbol is specially relevant here, but there is no
evidence for that knowledge. (On the other hand if the meaning is simply
"this woven spider-web," as Fraenkel takes it, then the symbolism lapses,
but that is weaker and less Aeschylean to my mind.) Possibly the reference
to the "Spider Mountain" in line 309 was a deliberate foreshadowing of
this.

**Lines 1497–1576**   The Chorus, being a male and not a female chorus,
dwell more on the legalistic aspects of the queen's crime than on their
sorrow for the king, though the repetition of the refrain and the additional
lamentation in ll. 1538–50 sustain a note of sorrow. Clytemnestra replies
mainly in legalistic terms. She shows a flash of her former imagination
in her sarcastic description of how Iphigeneia will, no doubt, fittingly
welcome Agamemnon's spirit in Hades with an embrace and a kiss. Her
vigorous defence reduces the Chorus again (cf. ll. 1530–32) to helplessness (*améchanía* l. 1561).

**Lines 1577–1611**   Joy, the evil joy of getting a brutal revenge—which
we are expected to dislike, not to share—returns for a moment with the
entry of Aigisthos and his invocation of "the kindly gleam of a day that
has brought justice." To justify his triumph he describes in ghastly detail
the abominable feast given to his father Thyestes by Agamemnon's father
Atreus. One word in his description offers another example of Aeschylus's

use of a brutal word to shock his hearers. Aigisthos says that when his father discovered that he was eating his own children's flesh he "vomited." The word used, *erôn*, does not occur elsewhere, nor do any of its cognates in Greek tragedy. In other instances of *stúgos* the reaction is to spit, as in line 1192. But here the reaction is literally more visceral, because the degree of revulsion is at the highest possible pitch. (The only other term in tragedy to equal the "coarseness" of this expression, together with *ataúrōtos* in line 244 and *histotríbēs* in line 1443, is the Nurses's reference to the "urine-letting" of the infant Orestes in *Libation-Bearers* line 756, but that is a matter of the Nurses's *êthos* rather than of any *páthos*.)

**Lines 1612–73**  The Chorus reacts with *némesis* and contempt to Aigisthos's rodomontade. Lloyd-Jones notes (l. 1624) that his constant use of trite sayings and comparisons (compare ll. 1617–20, 1628–32, 1641–42, 1668) helps to reveal the contemptible meanness of his character. Their scornful word for him, "Woman!" reverses the motif of the mannish woman that began in line 11. The notion of perversion is carried on, more ornamentally, in Aigisthos's reply: "Your tongue is the opposite of Orpheus's: he by his voice led everything after him in joy, but you by your puerile yelpings provoke hostility." As the interchanges of taunts and threats become more excited the iambic trimeters change to catalectic trochaic tetrameters (ll. 1649ff.)

Clytemnestra's attempt to make peace contains her strongest affirmation of affection in the play, when she says "Dearest of men" to Aigisthos. Her metaphor from reaping a harvest has nothing perverse about it. She attempts a reconciliation by addressing the chorus as "reverend elders," and by remarking, not ironically this time, I think, "That's a woman's saying if anyone thinks fit to learn from it." When she fails to stop the bickering, her impatience—as with Cassandra—flares up again, and with it her masterfulness: "Don't heed their futile yelpings. You and I, sharing the *krátos* over the House will settle things well." But, as the next play shows, the House and its curse are beyond their power to control.

The overall effect of this scene is to create a state of *taraché* which, together with the references to Orestes, keeps the audience in suspense for the next play of this integrated trilogy, just as in serial "thrillers" in the cinema each episode used to end at a moment of crisis. *Libation-Bearers* concludes with a similar state of *taragmós* in Orestes' mind and heart (l. 1056).

Looking back over the intense emotionalism of this play one may find clarification of its emotional vicissitudes in statistics (approximate because the references are not always definite). References to grief in general are by far the most frequent (about twenty-seven). Joy comes next with about twelve. Then come anger (nine), *philía* (eight), pity (seven), and *érōs* (six). Fear and hate have five appearances each, and next to them are anxiety, *stúgos, philanthrōpía, ékplēxis* (three each), *póthos, némesis, aidós, taraché* and an unspecified passion (two each). I leave it to others, if they wish, to make a fuller investigation of these frequencies with adequate discussion of the less definite references. But the general picture given here is, I believe, correct in outline, and it shows what a wide range of emotions is used in this the *Appassionata* of Aeschylus.

Some of the references are quite unemphatic. Others are emphasized by personification or extended descriptions, as we have seen. But even the least emphatic references could have an emotional effect subconsciously. Psychologists have studied the effect of subliminal advertisement in films or on television, when commercial slogans are flashed on the screen so fast that the eye cannot consciously perceive them, but—as some believe—the unconscious receives the message. In other words we can have, it is believed, perception without awareness. It may be, then, that the same principle holds in the audial sphere, so that even very brief references as, for example, those to *phthónos* in line 134 and to *némesis* (again by implication) in ll. 456–57 and 140–41, have a lasting effect.

The change to a female Chorus in *Libation-Bearers* enables Aeschylus to compensate for the rather brief lamentations of the Argive Elders in *Agamemnon* with a *kommós* that lasts for over a hundred and fifty lines (ll. 306–478). Besides grief, almost all the other main tragic emotions are given scope in this play—fear, anger, hate, disgust and joy. In the climactic scene when Clytemnestra bares her breast—the breast from which, as she pleads, Orestes had "drowsily drawn the nourishing milk with his gums" (ll. 896–98)—in the hope of escaping death at his hands, it is Orestes' necessary rejection of natural *storgé* for his mother that is most pitiful. Here the motif of perverted nature is taken from the queen and given to the prince. The same transference takes place with the recurrent symbolic image of the snake. In lines 249, 994 and 1047 the snake is Clytemnestra, as in Cassandra's description of her as an *amphísbaina* in *Agamemnon* line 1233. But in her dream as described in lines 526–34 the snake that draws blood from her breast must be Orestes. A clear analogy between this woman who kills her mate and is killed in turn by her offspring is noticed by Aelian in his treatise on the characteristics of animals when he describes (1.24) how the female viper (*échidna* as in ll. 249, 994) similarly kills and is killed. (Knowledge of this characteristic of vipers goes back at least to Herodotus 3.109.) Characteristically Aeschylus embodies these metaphorical serpents in the "thick-set snakes" of the Erinyes in line 1050. Finally, after the deaths of the queen and Aigisthos the third wave—or storm as the Chorus calls it in line 1066—has spent itself.

In the appearance of the Furies at the beginning of *Eumenides* all the earlier references to *stúgos* reach their climax, and all the metaphorical monsters are surpassed by these hideous, bloodthirsty, loathsome, fearsome, angry and ferocious creatures with their threats of atrocious diseases. In them, too, the sporadic metaphors from hunting in the earlier plays become part of the action and of the visual effects. Their conversion by Athene into "the Kindly Ones" is hardly plausible in terms of the arguments used, but it would be fully acceptable emotionally to Athenians in the optimistic atmosphere of the 450s B.C.

One emotional element in *Eumenides* is unique in Greek tragedy. This is the weird incantation, the "Binding Song" that is chanted and danced by the Furies in lines 307–96. In it Aeschylus plays on primitive fears of black magic and witchcraft as Shakespeare does in *Macbeth*—and both poets were dealing with audiences that fully believed in such things. (The modern equivalent might be a chorus of nuclear missiles or of cancer tumours.) Its audial effects reinforcing the fearsome conceptual meanings, deserve closer study than they have received as yet.

But the masterstroke of Aeschylean symbolical synthesis comes at the end of the trilogy when the vacillating imagery of light and darkness is consummated in a great crescendo of joy in lines 996ff., while the blood-coloured and blood-stained fabrics and robes of the two previous plays are sublimated in the red cloaks of the metics (see ll. 1018 and l. 1028, and compare *Agamemnon* l. 57 and *Libation-Bearers* l. 971). Similarly the "nestlings," both human and avian who suffered in the earlier plays (e.g., *Agamemnon* ll. 50f. and *Libation-Bearers* l. 256) have become the happy citizens of Athens gathered under the protective wings of their patron goddess in lines 1001–2.

The supreme glory of this finale is in its triumphant celebration of joy and illumination. There had been a false dawn at the end of *Libation-Bearers* when the Chorus sang "Now we can see the light" (l. 961), but the darkness soon returned. Here at long last we have the true radiance of lasting thanksgiving and gladness. Six times the Chorus and Athene cry "Be joyful" (*chaírete*), and the last words of the final refrain bring us back to the primeval way of expressing joy—"Cry aloud now at our songs-and-dances." We may well believe that all the Athenians in the audience shared these joyful cries and songs and dances in this magnificent affirmation of the civilizing power of their city. The effect is like that of the Hymn to Joy of Beethoven (and Schiller) at the end of his ninth and last symphony. But here the joy is expressed visually as well as audially, with *lumière* as well as *son*.

This is the happiest ending in all Greek tragedy, happiest for the characters in the play and happiest for the audience. It contains all the kinder emotions of tragedy—joy, *philanthrōpía*, love of one's native land, civic pride, and *elpís* in its good sense. It affirms that under the aegis of Athena—that is, under Athenian piety and democracy at their best—primitive blood feuds and monstrous crime will be banished by the rule of justice. Athenians could gladly believe this in 458 B.C. Sad that within a lifetime this belief was shattered when the Athenians forgot what Aeschylus had made the Chorus sing in *Agamemnon* ll. 381–84, "There is no shelter for a man when once in surfeit of wealth he has kicked the great altar of Justice into obscurity."

# No-Man's-Land of Dark and Light

*John Herington*

It may be well to recapitulate the main themes that have emerged from the *Suppliants* [in the first part of this essay, not reprinted here] and from the remains of the tetralogy to which it belonged. They are: the confrontation between male and female at all levels of the universe; the idea of a movement from violence toward a peaceful and creative concord, epitomized in the phrase "release from sorrow"; Zeus and his ambiguous nature; parallel to that ambiguity, the ambiguity in the character of the Danaid maidens; and the political upheaval in contemporary Athens. It may be said in advance that all these phenomena will be found to recur in the *Oresteia* or in the Prometheus plays or in both.

## ORESTEIA: AGAMEMNON

The *Oresteia* is an exemplary trinity. Simultaneously, it is both three, for each of its component plays can be, and often has been, staged as a separate artistic unit; and it is one, for there can be no comprehension of its full beauty and profundity until it is perceived as a unity. To stage *Agamemnon* on its own makes rather less sense than to perform the first movement of a Beethoven symphony on its own. The leading themes of the *Oresteia* are, it is true, introduced in *Agamemnon,* but in a confused and confusing way, for this play depicts a world in moral chaos, a world in which there seem to be no fixed principles left to hold on to. Those themes are clarified and separated out in the *Libation-Bearers,* but under

From *Aeschylus.* © 1986 by Yale University. Yale University Press, 1986.

conditions of at least equal hopelessness. The process of clarification, and the hopelessness too, persist in the *Eumenides*. Only in the last third of the last play are the themes finally orchestrated—into a hymn of joy that is no less startling in this context of tragedy than the intrusion of the human voice into an orchestra is in the last movement of the Ninth Symphony.

Correspondingly, as we should by now have come to expect of Aeschylus, the overall movement in this trilogy is from poetry heard to drama seen. *Agamemnon* is poetry heard for almost its entire length. Although it is far and away the longest of Aeschylus's surviving plays, the significant events that take place during its dramatic present can be described in a single sentence: The overlord of the Greeks, Agamemnon, returning from the Trojan War to his palace in Argos, is there murdered by his wife Clytaemnestra, abetted by her lover, Aegisthus. Yet not only does the central incident of the murder occur offstage, out of the audience's sight (throughout Attic tragedy, with only a few partial exceptions, the civilized convention persists that acts of violence must not be represented onstage), it is even unfocused, as it were, in time; for it is seen and described by the seeress Cassandra some minutes before it actually happens (ll. 1100–35, compare ll. 1223–46). That blurring of edges is in fact characteristic of the whole drama. *Agamemnon* is a play of ambiguities; and in Aeschylus ambiguity is primarily the domain of the spoken word.

By far the greatest part of the play is devoted to the pursuit of the two interlinked questions: what were the sequences of events that led up to the murder? And on whose side did justice lie? As far as line 781, the speaking and the singing are preoccupied with a meditation on the guilt incurred in the Trojan War. We hear of the guilt of Paris, who lured Helen away from her husband, Menelaus, to live with him in Troy; of Menelaus and his elder brother Agamemnon, who did not shrink from causing a terrible war in order to bring one woman home; but above all of Agamemnon himself, who cruelly sacrificed his and Clytaemnestra's daughter Iphigenia to obtain a fair wind for the Greek armada as it waited to set out, and then, after finally conquering Troy, simply obliterated it— people, walls, altars, temples, the very seeds that lay hidden beneath its soil (ll. 525–28). By the moment of Agamemnon's triumphal entrance into the theater at line 782, he appears about as guilty as a man could be—guilty as a commander and guilty as a father and husband. Yet a further token of his guilt is embodied in the seeress Cassandra, who rides in his procession; she is not only a representative of the many Trojan women who were enslaved after the sack, but she has also been taken by Agamemnon as his mistress. On her, in fact, hinges the transition to the second sequence of causes that lead to Agamemnon's murder. In her superb scene from line 1072 to line 1330, she penetrates with her second sight into both the past and future horrors that lie within the palace walls, and in so doing reveals a side of Clytaemnestra that up to now has been hinted at only in riddles: on Clytaemnestra too lies guilt, for what she has done and for what she is about to do. This technique . . . of representing a character in contradictory aspects and revealing only gradually which is the true face, is richly exploited throughout the *Oresteia;* probably the most spectacular example will be found toward its end, in Aeschylus's handling of the Furies in the *Eumenides.*

From the Cassandra scene onward, the play's emphasis shifts to the causes, near and remote, that led Clytaemnestra to her act of murder. Near is her adulterous love affair, during Agamemnon's long absence, with his cousin Aegisthus. Remote was a vendetta that had begun in the preceding generation. Atreus (father of Agamemnon and Menelaus) and his brother Thyestes had long feuded over the lordship of Argos. At last Atreus invited Thyestes into the palace—the same palace in front of which *Agamemnon* is set—on the pretense of a reconciliation. At the welcoming feast he fed the flesh of Thyestes' own butchered children to him. On discovering what the food was, Thyestes pronounced a great curse on the entire family. Atreus then drove him into exile, and with him the only one of his children who had escaped the butchery, an infant, Aegisthus. And none other than Aegisthus is the last character to make an entrance in *Agamemnon.* His epiphany culminates visually the meditation on the second sequence of crimes, very much as Agamemnon's epiphany, earlier, had culminated the meditation on the first.

The search for causes and justifications which thus dominated the play naturally entails a vast sweep outward and backward from the dramatic place and dramatic time at which *Agamemnon* is set. If the audience was to assess the true moral implications of the murder, it would ideally need to be transported to prewar Troy as it welcomed Helen into the city, for instance, or to the Argive palace at the moment when the smiling Atreus watched the meal being set before his brother. That kind of free movement through time and space, or something very close to it, was long after to be conferred on dramatists by the invention of cinematography. But already Aeschylus's verbal poetry, if rightly listened to, is capable of producing very nearly the same effects; and in *Agamemnon,* by every reader's experience, his verbal poetry reaches its supreme heights.

We have already mentioned one or two examples of that poetry's power to transport the spectator just beyond the physical limits of the stage setting: the Shield Scene in the *Seven against Thebes* and Danaus's description of the arrival of the Egyptian squadron in the *Suppliants*. In *Agamemnon*, however, it soars effortlessly from the palace at Argos, over the mountains to the east, across the Aegean sea to the Hellespont and Troy, bringing back word pictures so vivid that they fix themselves in the mind's eye scarcely less than in the ear. One remembers as clearly as if they had been physically staged the preparations for the sacrifice of Iphigenia, described entirely in song in the latter part of the opening chorus (ll. 223–47)—not least, perhaps, the appalling detail of the piteous look in the little girl's eyes during her last moments of life, after Agamemnon had ordered his attendants to gag her; or Clytaemnestra's pictures of Troy in the dawn light immediately after its fall (ll. 320–37): the crude disharmony of voices as the conquered wail and the conquerors cry out for joy; the pathetic little heaps formed by the living Trojan young who have fallen across the corpses of the old; and the Greek soldiers jostling to find a breakfast and a good billet now that the night's work is over. Likewise one remembers the Herald's account of the common soldier's life in the Greek forward outposts during the long siege (ll. 558–66), so much closer to the eternal realities of military life than anything to be found in Homer: the ever-present damp, the rotting uniforms, the lice, the "bird-killing cold" of winter, and the murderous heat of the summer days, when the Hellespont "Waveless and windless dozed in its noonday rest."

Yet it is Helen, perhaps, who abides most clearly in one's memory after a reading of *Agamemnon*, even though she never physically appears in the play. Here are two glimpses of her, and of what she meant. In the choral passage from line 403 to line 426 we are told how Menelaus felt after she had left him; lines 414–26 run somewhat like this:

> Yearning for a woman,
> A woman over sea,
> He shall think the ghost of her
> Is true master in his house.
> The charm of statues carved in her perfect form
> Shall rouse his hate. When the living eyes are lost,
> Any love is ended.
>
> Sad fancies shining out of dreams
> Are about him still, to offer hollow joy.

He touches her?
—Straightway the vision flitting through his arms
Is gone, lightly on wings down the trails of sleep.

And here is a vision of Helen on her arrival at Troy:

When she first came, I should call her
The thought of peace at sea when the winds are down,
Gentle arrow of the eyes,
Stingheart flower of love!

(ll. 737–42)

In relatively few lyric lines (one should add lines 681–749 and 1455–60 to what I have quoted above), Aeschylus creates out of words alone a Helen of Troy quite as lovely and as demonic as most of the Helens who have actually walked on the stage in later dramas. But these passages have not been composed just as virtuoso feats to be admired in passing, brilliant though they are. Helen is an integral part of the moral texture of *Agamemnon*. We must stand in her magnificent presence for a while if we are to comprehend the full cause and significance of the king's murder. And, through Aeschylus's poetry, we do so stand.

Another equally important aspect of Aeschylus's art in *Agamemnon* (and indeed, in this case, in the *Oresteia* as a whole) may be introduced through the play's prologue. The opening words of any Aeschylean drama, but above all of this one, need to be listened to with the same concentration as that with which one listens to the first measures of a Bach fugue. The speech that the weary Watchman delivers in the predawn darkness from the roof of Agamemnon's palace embodies many themes that will be developed in surprising ways from one end of the trilogy to the other, some of them even emerging into visible form. In the following translation of *Agamemnon* lines 1–22, I have italicized the most significant of those themes:

I ask the Gods *deliverance from these pains,*
This watching; for a whole year's length I have lain
Muzzle to paws, doglike, on the Atreids' roof,
Learning to know the parliament of night—
Those stars who bring the seasons, cold and heat,
Bright lords in splendor set against the sky.
    And still I watch for the *signal of the light,*
For the *glare of fire* to bring the news from Troy,
Shouting her fall!

Those are my orders, issued
By *a woman who plans in her male heart,* and waits.
My bed is no bed, restless through the night
And damp with dew. No *dreams* can visit there,
For fear, not sleep, is all my company.
I cannot ever firmly close my eyes.
   Sometimes I think I'll sing or hum, to cure
My sleepiness by the medicine of music—
But then instead I weep, I mourn aloud
For this house and its state; it is no longer
Managed as excellently as it was of old.
   Now come, happy *deliverance from pains,*
The *fire in blackness* flaring its glad news!
   [He gestures as if he has seen the beacon far
   offstage.]
Welcome, you *lamp of night shining as day!*

These lines, like the rest of the Watchman's speech, and indeed like much of *Agamemnon,* are of the stuff of nightmare. The shifting, contradictory imagery—light out of darkness, day out of night, the female with the male heart—are matched by shifting, contradictory emotions, hope and terror, the urge to sing that melts into weeping. Opening and closing the passage that precedes the Watchman's sighting of the beacon is a prayer of deliverance from pains. Eventually that will be understood, in fact, to have struck the keynote for the entire trilogy, but not until the last few minutes of its performance. In the interim, again in nightmare fashion, deliverance will retreat further and further with each step the characters seem to take toward it. The light the simple Watchman believes to herald it will soon prove to be more terrifying than the darkness out of which it issued, for it bears not only the news of victory at Troy but also a signal to the waiting Queen Clytaemnestra that the time has arrived to prepare for murder. Several times the characters who appear later in *Agamemnon* will salute the day, or the light, or Justice (*Dikē*), or all three, as if the speaker's cause has been finally vindicated and the slate of ancient crime and suffering has been wiped clean. "Agamemnon comes," says the Herald (ll. 521–26), "bringing us light in our nighttime. . . . Greet him, who has dug Troy into the ground with the pickaxe of Justice-bearing Zeus!" When Agamemnon himself arrives, his first words are (ll. 810–14): "First it is justice to address Argos and the Gods who live in her, who helped me to come home, and to exact just punishment from the city of Priam; for the Gods heard my unspoken pleas for justice." After the murder has been done, Clytaemnestra cries to the Chorus (ll. 1432–36): "Now, by the justice that has been fulfilled for my daughter [Iphigenia], I swear to you that my expectation does not tread within Fear's palace, so long as I have Aegisthus like a blazing fire upon my hearth." And when Aegisthus finally shows himself upon the stage, his first line is (l. 1577): "O kindly light of justice-bearing day!"

That is only one image-cluster of many that run through the trilogy, and only one illustration of the moral confusion that reigns in *Agamemnon*. Each party in turn claims that justice is on his or her side and that the light shines for him or her alone. But for Agamemnon and the Herald, as for Clytaemnestra and Aegisthus, light and justice will prove to be no more than will-o'-the-wisps, phantoms that, like the dream of Helen, will soon be off and away, "lightly on wings down the trails of sleep." No certainties are left in the world, except the certainty that crime means more crime. As the Chorus sings toward the end of the great scene (ll. 1412–1576) in which they and Clytaemnestra together review all the possible causes and justifications of the murder, both human and divine,

> It is a losing battle to decide,
> For ravaged ravages again,
> And murderer pays murder's price.

Even the two visual tableaux that *Agamemnon* contains, although among the most famous dramatic spectacles in Greek tragedy, do not solve any mysteries in the way that Aeschylean tableaux are elsewhere apt to do. Rather, they make plain to the eye once and for all the reality, first of Agamemnon's guilt, then of Clytaemnestra's. Taken as a responding pair, as they are surely designed to be, they simply emphasize the moral dilemma around which the play is built. In the episode that has come to be known as the Tapestry Scene (ll. 905–74), where Clytaemnestra tempts Agamemnon not to set his foot on this common earth but to approach the palace over purple cloths that she has had her servants lay from the chariot to the palace door, the arrogance and folly in the heart of Troy's conqueror are given magnificent external expression. Knowing as he well does that such an honor should be reserved for the gods alone, he at last lets himself be persuaded to walk that purple path and to go through the door to his eventual death. For a moment, the opening in the *skēnē* with its protruding purple tongue may remind us of the Hell-Mouth in a mediaeval mystery play; and that indeed is very close to its meaning here. The second great tableau occurs abruptly at line 1372, where that same palace door swings open to reveal Clytaemnestra standing over her husband's corpse. The body lies in a silver bath (as is shown by lines 1539–40), still wrapped in the folds of the great cloth in which she entangled him before stabbing him (ll. 1382–84, 1492, 1580). Visible also is the body of the slaughtered Cassandra (l. 1440). The corpses can be seen throughout Clytaemnestra's inconclusive debate with the Chorus about the causes of the murder, and are still there for Aegisthus to gloat over at his entrance (ll. 1581–82). No doubt they remain on view until the end of the play, mute witnesses to Clytaemnestra's crime.

*Agamemnon* then, brings us no certainties, religious or moral or even emotional—the manic-depressive swings of mood that we noted already in the Watchman are experienced also, for instance, by the Chorus (lines 99–103 offer a striking example). No certainties; only, here and there, flareups of intuition into truths which will be slowly justified in practice as the trilogy unfolds. One such intuitional flareup, it seems to me, is the passage lines 160–83, which is probably the most famous song that Aeschylus ever composed. In modern times it has come to be referred to, almost as if it were an independent poem, as the "Hymn to Zeus," and indeed at a first hearing it may well appear to have little enough to do with its immediate context in the Chorus's great opening chant and song (lines 40–257, the longest uninterrupted choral utterance in Attic tragedy). As a whole, that chant and song are devoted to a vision of the preliminaries to the sailing of the expedition to Troy. The Chorus recalls (ll. 104–59) the omen of the pair of eagles feasting on a pregnant hare, which the army-seer Calchas interpreted—and this is characteristic of the mood of the entire play—as simultaneously favorable and terrible: in the knot of writhing creatures he sees that Agamemnon and Menelaus will succeed in annihilating Troy, but that this act may bring upon them the anger of the goddess of all natural life, Artemis. The second major episode of the song (ll. 184–257) lyrically narrates the immediate result of her anger: she caused contrary winds to blow where the fleet was moored at Aulis, and would not let it sail until Agamemnon sacrificed his own daughter to her. Interposed between these two ominous narratives, like a desperate cry for help out of the moral abyss, is the Hymn to Zeus.

The Zeus invoked here, like the second of the two facets of Zeus recognized in the *Suppliants,* is a mysterious being of immense power. The Chorus is not even sure of his right name (ll. 160–62); it only knows, like the Danaid chorus, that he is its sole hope of release from sorrow. For this is the God who has

> Brought human beings on the road to wisdom
> By setting firm this law:
> *Through suffering, learning!*
> At the heart's gate, even in sleep,
> Agony of remembered pain
> Falls drop by drop, and even to the unwilling
> Come wisdom and restraint.
> And do the Spirits who sit at the august helm
> Through violence show their kindness?
>
> (ll. 176–83)

Since Byzantine times this intuition of a Zeus who guides mankind to righteousness through chastisement has reminded commentators of the message of the Old Testament. But even while we wonder at that resemblance, it is important to bear in mind certain differences too. First, taken in its dramatic context this passage is not to be understood (as it often seems to be) as Aeschylus's personal statement of a creed guaranteed by divine revelation. It is a point of view expressed by the old men of the Chorus—a hope, which they do not try to justify either by revelation or by experience. Second, this Zeus, like the transcendent Zeus invoked by the Danaids and unlike the God of the Old Testament, has a past behind him—a violent mythological past, which is alluded to in the second of the hymn's three stanzas. He wrestled down the previous lord of the universe, his own father, Kronos, who himself had dethroned *his* father, Ouranos; Heaven too has once known the chaos of the vendetta, just as humanity knows it now, at the dramatic time of *Agamemnon.* For the interpreter of the art of the *Oresteia,* the main significance of the Hymn to Zeus is that, at this early and desperate stage of the story, it introduces the ideas that human beings may *learn,* even at the cost of great agony, and that even the gods may, if not change, at least ultimately reveal a different face. Both ideas are in fact eventually realized in the progress of the trilogy, as is the Watchman's prayer for "deliverance from pains." The technique is basically the same as that which we have already witnessed in the *Persians,* where the elders' intuition into the laws of the archaic universe, expressed in their opening song, is only later corroborated by actual events; the difference is that the time-lapse between intuition and corroboration is far longer in the *Oresteia,* on account of its far greater scale.

Less generally noticed than the Hymn to Zeus, but perhaps no less marvelous an example of this technique, is another premonitory passage that occurs later in *Agamemnon*. At lines 1372–98 Clytaemnestra, stand-ing over the two corpses, recalls moment by moment not merely the murder of Agamemnon but also her sensations as she committed it. Here is an attempt to render the culminating lines of that speech:

> I strike him twice, and in a double scream
> He lets his limbs collapse. As he lies there,
> I throw in a third stab, to carry down
> My vow to Zeus our Savior under Earth
> —Zeus, Savior of corpses! So he falls
> And speeds away the spirit of his being,
> And puffing out a sudden spurt of gore
> Hits me with a dark shower of blood-red rain
> —And I rejoice, just as the seeded fields
> Delight in the liquid joy bestowed by heaven
> At the childbearing of the buds in spring!
>
> (ll. 1384–92)

This speech is riddled with blasphemy. Zeus in his aspect of Savior or Preserver, *Sōtēr*, was the deity to whom the Greeks customarily poured the third of the three ritual wine libations that opened a festive drinking-party or *symposion*. Here Clytaemnestra tauntingly transforms Zeus into his ghastly counterpart, Hades, lord of the dead (here one may well recall the blasphemous threat of the Danaids in *Suppliants* lines 154–75), and her libation is offered not in wine but in blood. But the image expressed in the last four lines quoted, the image that crossed her mind as Aga-memnon's blood spurted over her, seems to imply the worst blasphemy of all. It is evidently a perversion of the primaeval myth of the mating of Heaven and Earth in the spring rains, which we heard from the mouth of Aphrodite in the *Danaides*. In that myth the primal Male came together with the primal Female in the mutual joy of creation. Clytaemnestra, however, after that third and wanton blow, seems to have cast Agamem-non in the role of Heaven and herself in the role of Earth, while the spurt of blood stood for the gentle falling of the rain/semen; she transformed the ancient world's supreme symbol of love between the sexes into her own supreme symbol of hatred. In the moment of murdering her hus-band, she intuited something more terrifying even than murder: a uni-verse divided by open war between the male and the female. That intuition will become closer and closer to reality—onstage reality—in the course of the *Libation-Bearers* and the *Eumenides*.

ORESTEIA: LIBATION-BEARERS

On the face of it, the *Libation-Bearers* might seem to be a revenge play of the type quite familiar in the later European dramatic tradition. Students have often compared it to *Hamlet,* and indeed one will notice some fascinating resemblances between the two plays. Even more interesting, however, are the *differences* between the two playwrights' treatments of the theme of the prince who avenges his father's murder. Just one of those differences may be mentioned here, but that one alone will illuminate the uniqueness of Aeschylean tragedy by comparison with any tragedy that was to come. Hamlet proceeds to his revenge through a long-protracted agony of internal conflict. Orestes, having once reunited himself with his sister and secured the support of his dead father's spirit, proceeds to *his* revenge with swift and relentless efficiency; only after the murder does his personality fall apart, and then because it is violently invaded by a force from outside. Only then, also, does it begin to appear that in the *Libation-Bearers* we have been witnessing not merely an individual human being's act of vengeance, but the drawing of the lines in a cosmic conflict.

The action of the play, quite unlike that of *Agamemnon,* lies almost entirely in the dramatic here and now. There are few of those wide sweeps into distant places and the past on the wings of verbal poetry. Indeed, all the significant incidents in this plot which tragic convention permitted to be enacted onstage—that is, all except the actual murders—take place before the audience's eyes. It is in this respect (but perhaps, on reflection, one may think *only* in this respect) that the *Libation-Bearers* anticipates the effects of drama as drama has been understood from Sophocles onward more than any play of Aeschylus that we have seen so far. Especially in the scenes from line 652 (where Orestes presents himself at the palace door) until the end, the stage action moves as fast and as excitingly as it does in any modern thriller-play. I shall review the *Libation-Bearers* first in that strictly dramatic aspect. After that, I shall explore the poetic means by which Aeschylus, as the human revenge-story progresses, gradually clarifies the confused themes announced in *Agamemnon* and simultaneously prepares for the ultimate clarifications of the *Eumenides.*

This is how the revenge for Agamemnon's murder is brought about on the human plane: Orestes, under stringent orders from Apollo to execute that revenge (lines 269–305), returns to Argos from the Delphic territory of Phocis, to which his mother Clytaemnestra has sent him long ago, before the murder. With him is his Phocian friend, Pylades, a silent presence throughout except at lines 900–902, where he intervenes at a climactic moment almost with the voice of the Delphic Apollo himself; but he is a constant visual reminder of Apollo's commitment to the vengeance. Orestes' first action is to pay homage at Agamemnon's tomb (represented by a mound in the center of the *orchēstra*?), laying on it a lock of his hair as an offering due to Inachus, the river god of his native land, and another lock in mourning for Agamemnon. His devotions are interrupted by the entrance of his sister Electra and the Chorus, consisting of captive women, who are also bringing offerings to the tomb in the form of libations. The two men withdraw out of sight of the procession, while the grim tomb-ritual takes its course. It soon appears from the women's words that Clytaemnestra has ordered these belated rites to be observed as the result of an ominous dream (lines 32–46).

Just after Electra has poured the libations at the tomb-mound, she notices the lock and the footprints left there by Orestes and concludes from the resemblances to her own hair and feet that they must be his. At that point Orestes steps forward and finally convinces her of his identity by showing her another token—a piece of cloth that he carries woven by Electra in her childhood long ago. The sheer unrealism of this recognition scene, by any ordinary standards of logic, has been noted by Aeschylus's critics ever since Euripides, who less than half a century later exposed it with wicked humor in his *Electra* (ll. 508–45). It is yet another reminder of the gulf that separates Aeschylus from any later tragedian. One cannot enforce ordinary realistic standards on these characters of his, who are both more and less than ordinary individuals, who exist on the borderline between life as we know it and a mythical, demonic world. In that world, as in a fairy-tale or a nightmare, the incongruous or the impossible may make better sense than any petty realities, as symbols of a deeper intuited truth. Of course, it is implausible that a sister, by comparing an unknown lock of hair and a set of footprints with her own hair and feet, should know instantly that they belong to her brother and no one else in the world; while obviously any stranger, even an enemy bent on betraying Electra, might somehow have acquired that piece of weaving. Yet there could hardly be any more powerful symbols than those for their bond as sister and brother, two alone against the wide world. In evaluating this and many other scenes in Aeschylus, we might do better to apply the criteria of surrealism than those of realism.

There remains a third family member who must be drawn into the reunion before the vengeance can proceed. It is, again, characteristic of the Aeschylean vision that Orestes, Electra, and the Chorus have still to

exert all their powers in order to bring the spirit of Agamemnon to their
aid from the recesses of Earth. They do so by means of a tremendous
chant, dance, and song around the funeral mound (ll. 306–478), which
is the most elaborately composed operatic scene in Aeschylus's surviving
work and, as such, unfortunately, the most difficult to translate into two-
dimensional English verse, as it were; here more than anywhere the reader
needs imaginatively to bring the flat text up into its original rhythm,
melody, and spectacle. The chanting and singing lead into an antiphony
in unaccompanied spoken verse between Orestes and Electra (ll. 479–
509), in which their incantation rises to a desperate urgency, as if the
sheer force of words might compel the dead king out of his grave:

> ORESTES: Send up, O Earth, my father to watch over this bat-
> tle!
> ELECTRA: And grant, Persephone, victory's lovely form! . . .
> ORESTES: My father, are you now waking at this tale of your
> dishonor?
> ELECTRA: Are you now raising up your much-loved head?

Anyone who had watched the *Persians* fourteen years earlier might well
have been in fearful suspense by this point: would the ghastly figure of
the murdered man now slowly rise out of the mound, as the serene ghost
of Darius had risen after a similar but in fact much shorter tomb-ritual?
But here Aeschylus deludes our expectations; this is not yet the time in
the trilogy for the supernatural powers to be manifested to the eye, only
for them to press closer and closer against the flimsy curtain which separates them from living humanity.

After the ritual is over, Orestes is further emboldened by the
Chorus's description of the nightmare that had impelled Clytaemnestra
to send the procession to the tomb (ll. 514–22): the dread vision of a
snake to which she gave suck and which in that process bit into her breast,
drawing blood along with the mother's milk. Thus, now triply armed
with the protection of Apollo, the power of his father's spirit, and the
portent that has emerged out of the darkness of his mother's mind,
Orestes is at last ready to lay his plans for the murder, as he does in
lines 555–84. He and his silent companion, Pylades, leave the scene
through one of the side passages, while Electra withdraws into the palace.
The theatral area is left to the Chorus, which now sings that ode, part
of which was quoted earlier, on the destructive powers that lie within the
human heart, and especially within the heart of Woman.

The action that follows the central ode moves before our eyes with
remarkable speed until the end of the play. Even the sung and chanted

interventions of the Chorus are no longer the lengthy, far-ranging lyric meditations to which we have been used so far in Aeschylus's work, but relatively short and businesslike, being directly involved with the action at hand; the song at lines 783–837, for instance, has practically the effect of a war dance, putting heart into Orestes for the kill. Orestes, for his part, wastes very little time. At line 652 he and Pylades, both in the disguise of Phocian travelers, appear at the palace door, to which the focus of the play's action now shifts from the tomb-mound. (Aeschylus was no slave to what was later called "the Unity of Place": a similar shift of focus, this time *to* a tomb, has already been seen in the *Persians,* and very much more drastic ones will occur in the *Eumenides.*) They are greeted by Clytaemnestra in person, whom Orestes persuades by a plausible story that he, Orestes, has lately died in his Phocian exile. She has the apparent strangers conducted into the men's quarters of the palace, and herself withdraws in order to see that her lord, Aegisthus, is informed of the news.

But Clytaemnestra's caution and resourcefulness have not deserted her, even when to all appearances that last possible threat to her and Aegisthus's security has been removed by Orestes' death. This we learn indirectly from the next person to enter, the old slave-woman Cilissa, who nursed Orestes in his infancy. Clytaemnestra, she says, has sent her out to tell Aegisthus to come and hear the strangers' story, adding the instruction that he must come not alone but with his bodyguard. The Chorus narrowly saves the conspirators from total failure there and then by persuading the innocent old woman to leave out the second part of that message. The Cilissa scene (ll. 734–82) illustrates a dimension of Aeschylus's art that appears in the *Oresteia* alone of his extant plays: its capacity to characterize the common man with sympathy and even tenderness. The speeches of the Watchman and the Herald in *Agamemnon* offer many hints of this quite unexpected side of our poet—unexpected, that is, to anyone who has not read the fragments and who has approached the extant plays, as we have done, in chronological order (contrast, for instance, the speeches of the Messengers in the *Persians* and the *Seven against Thebes*). But it is Cilissa who stands out from this point of view. Amid the schemings, the hypocrisies, and the demonic passions of the princes, which are richly exemplified in the scenes on either side of this one, she stands desolated by simple, unaffected sorrow at the news of Orestes' supposed death. She can see the hero only as the baby whom she loved with all her heart, even though his screams troubled her nights, and though his soiled clothing cost her endless labor at the washtub (ll. 748–63).

Thus Aegisthus arrives without any attendants and unsuspectingly enters the door of the men's quarters. His murder follows after a very short interval, being signaled to the audience by a scream offstage (1. 869; one does not miss the symmetry between the effects here and those at the moment of Agamemnon's murder). One of his servants rushes out to summon Clytaemnestra, who presently enters, to be faced by Orestes and Pylades. At this culmination of his plot Orestes falters only for one moment, and that is when his mother points to the breast with which she suckled him as an infant and appeals to him to revere it. Confronted in this most elemental way with the full meaning of what he has set out to do, he turns to Pylades for advice; and Pylades speaks for the first and only time in the play (ll. 900–902), sternly reminding him of his obligation to Apollo's oracle and to the gods. There is an end to hesitation: step by step, it seems, to the accompaniment of a line-by-line interchange between them (ll. 908–28), the son forces the mother back through the palace door. During that drawn-out retreat toward inevitable death she threatens him with a mother's curse, expressing it in line 924 in the shape of a riddling warning:

Look now, beware of your mother's spiteful hounds!

Their disappearance, followed by Pylades, into that doom-laden palace door is followed by a triumph-song from the Chorus. Then, at line 973, the door swings open again to display Orestes, with Pylades, standing over the corpses of Clytaemnestra and Aegisthus. The awesome tableau, of course, corresponds to the tableau revealed at *Agamemnon* line 1372 and results, for the moment, in a sense of completed symmetry, a sense of an ending. The clear message to the audience's eyes, as well as to its mind, is that the age-old law of retaliation has been fulfilled, and the family vendetta has reached the point where no human avengers are left. But the final scene of the *Libation-Bearers* (ll. 973–1076) will transform all. Before proceeding to it, however, it will be well to turn for a while from the surface action of the play to consider the means by which Aeschylus has all along been unobtrusively leading up to that last and most terrible revelation.

The mood of the *Libation-Bearers* is visually set from the first by the black costumes in which the Chorus members are dressed (1. 11). Indeed, from their entrance until very near the end of the *Oresteia* as whole (as will be seen later), the theater is dominated by the great black rectangle composed by the successive choruses of women and of Furies. Morally, too, the trilogy is progressing ever deeper into blackness. Here and there the verbal imagery, as in *Agamemnon,* offers a flare of light; but, also as in *Agamemnon,* the light's message will prove a delusion. The instances are worth recalling before we proceed to that final scene of our play. On a probable reading of the Greek text, Electra at line 131 begs the dead Agamemnon to "kindle Orestes as a light in our house"; just before Aegisthus's murder the Chorus prays (ll. 808–10) that "the light of Freedom may look on Orestes," showing its "kindly eyes from out the veil of darkness"; and in its song during Clytaemnestra's murder the refrain is twice heard, "the light is here to see!" As with light, so with justice, which was so often associated with it in *Agamemnon.* Throughout our play the murder of Clytaemnestra is represented by the conspirators as the fulfillment of justice. Thus, early on, Electra prays at the tomb (l. 144) "that those who killed may die through justice in return," and the Chorus, in the song during Clytaemnestra's murder that was just quoted, proclaims (ll. 948–51) that Justice, the daughter of Zeus, "breathing mortal rage against our enemies," has laid her hand on that of Orestes in this struggle.

On the whole, therefore, the idea of justice which prevails in the *Libation-Bearers* is no different from that which prevailed in the previous play. It continues to be equated with the iron law of retaliation, just as it was by the Herald, Agamemnon, Clytaemnestra, and Aegisthus in turn, and its seeming fulfillment is still seen as the light of salvation. Where Orestes and Electra differ from the actors of *Agamemnon,* in fact, is not in their perception of justice, but in the spirit in which they execute it. They show none of the cruel satisfaction with which the Herald and Agamemnon spoke of the justice dealt out to Troy, still less the unholy ecstasy which the king's murder inspired in Clytaemnestra and Aegisthus, Electra, indeed, in the very speech at the tomb in which she prays for the return and vengeance of Orestes, includes the prayer (ll. 140–41); "and for myself, grant that I may be far more chaste than my mother, and more pious in my acts." The brother and sister seem to possess an intuition, still unformulated, of a justice that transcends revenge. And yet the murder, the murder of a mother by her son, must still be carried out. Apollo, the Olympian deity of the light, has ordered it and guaranteed Orestes his protection. Orestes' murdered father has been summoned from the grave to his support. On three levels of being—divine, human, and infernal—the male has been aligning its forces to crush a woman—or is Clytaemnestra to be thought of just as an individual woman? Remembering her perception of herself at the moment she stabbed her husband, we may wonder. But not until the last scene of the

*Libation-Bearers* is there any further hint that on her side, too, an array of powers is being lined up, this time female powers.

To return at last to that scene: the tableau revealed at line 973 is both a counterpart and a contrast to the tableau of *Agamemnon* line 1372. Again the slayer stands over the slain, but Orestes is carrying the garlanded bough (l. 1035) that proclaims him to be a suppliant of Apollo. Shortly afterward, in another of the magnificent visual gestures of the *Oresteia,* he has his attendants stretch out the great, still bloodstained cloth in which Agamemnon was entangled at his murder, and show it to the sunlight, as justification for his act. There is no triumph in his words: only, first, an almost hysterial condemnation of his mother's wickedness, then a realization (l. 1017) of the depth of the pollution that he has incurred, then (l. 1021) an admission that his mind is violently swerving beyond the bounds of sanity. He only has time, before madness strikes, to claim once more the patronage of Apollo, knowing that his only hope now is to reach the temple at Delphi and its "undying light of fire" (l. 1037); yet once again in the trilogy the elusive light has flickered away into the far distance. Suddenly (l. 1048) he lets out a great scream. Visible to him alone, the female supernatural powers are moving in on him; they appear to him as a swarm of Gorgon-like women, black-clothed, with snakes entangled in their hair and blood oozing from their eyes. As yet he can give them no name—neither he nor the audience, in fact, will be certain about that until well into the following play—but at least he can now solve the riddle that Clytaemnestra posed as she retreated to the palace door: "these are my mother's spiteful hounds, clear to the eye" (l. 1054; cf. l. 924). As he rushes from the scene to try to escape them, the Chorus, unwittingly echoing the thought of the Watchman at the very beginning of the trilogy, assure him that "Apollo will set you free from these sorrows" (ll. 1059–60). After he has vanished, however, their feelings are less confident. In their recessional chant they reflect on the interminability of blood-feud. First came the banquet served by Atreus to Thyestes, then the murder of Agamemnon, and now?

> Now for the third time has arrived from somewhere
> A Savior—or should I call him Doom?
> Where will it consummate,
> Where will it rest and fall asleep at last,
> The spirit of destruction?

Even the Chorus has seen at the last that the old justice and the old light have failed. The vendetta has not ended. As will be revealed more clearly in the final play of the *Oresteia,* it is to continue on a vaster scale, involving the fundamental powers in the universe and human life as we experience it: the male and the female.

ORESTEIA: EUMENIDES

*Eumenides* stands to the rest of the *Oresteia* somewhat as the epiphany of Darius in the *Persians* stands to all that has gone before in that play. The supernatural takes visible shape, and with that manifestation all doubts are dispelled. In its light we can at last make sense of the mysteries in the human story that has been told so far. But in the *Persians,* as we saw, the divine epiphany occupied only a single episode, and it revealed a static universe at peace with itself, its harmony disturbed only by the transgression of mortal pride. The epiphany of the *Eumenides* occupies an entire play, and it is a progressive revelation of a universe in the midst of violent change. The drama and its suspense continue, but they continue partly on to the divine plane. Almost from the first we are made to realize with the utmost clarity something that we may have surmised toward the end of the *Libation-Bearers* and something that Clytaemnestra had already intuited as she murdered Agamemnon: at stake in the human feud which has unfolded in the two earlier plays is nothing less than the relationship between male and female throughout the universe.

In the rapid succession of scenes at Delphi (ll. 1–235), the representatives of the male and female divine forces appear before our eyes in bitter enmity with each other. And they are, indeed, only representatives. Apollo speaks with the voice of Zeus (this is stressed three times, at lines 19, 615–18, and 713), and hence of the Olympian patriarchy (l. 618); the Furies invoke as their allies two of the oldest female deities in the cosmos—Night (ll. 321–22, 416, 745, 792, 822, 845, 877) and Fate, alternatively referred to as the Fates (ll. 172, 335, 392, 961). It is significant that in this play Aeschylus differs from all other recorded Greek genealogies of the gods by making the Furies the daughters of Night, who is Fate's sister (ll. 961–62). By so doing he both elevates their cosmic status and directly associates them with darkness; and indeed, darkness or blackness prove to be characteristic both of the Furies and of the feminine generally. The Furies' costumes are black (l. 370; cf. *Libation-Bearers* l. 1049), like those of the women in the Chorus of the *Libation-Bearers,* and line 52 may even imply that their masks and limbs are black also. They dwell in the darkness below earth (ll. 72 and 395), in a gloom that knows no sunlight (l. 396, cf. ll. 386–87). Athena, says Apollo, did not come to being "in the darkness of the womb" (1. 665); on the other hand, as Orestes claims, Clytaemnestra's "thoughts were black" (1. 459).

At last, then, the confused imagery of light and dark that has pervaded the trilogy since the Watchman's opening speech is, as it were, polarized and actually presented to the eye. Light (male, heavenly, patriarchal) is flatly opposed to darkness (female, earthly, matriarchal). So long as this rift endures there can be no hope of creation in any sense or at any level. The fruits of the earth will not grow, cattle will not multiply, neither families nor larger societies will hold together. All these consequences, as we shall see, are increasingly stressed in the latter half of the *Eumenides*. The universe is in peril of a state opposite to that envisaged in Aphrodite's picture of the ultimate sexual union in the *Danaides*. In the *Oresteia*, it seems, as in that earlier trilogy on the fate of the Danaids, Aeschylus is still preoccupied with the human male-female relationship as a symbol that will illuminate the workings of the cosmos. Here, however, its symbolism takes on political, legal, and social dimensions as well. One of the most surprising features of the *Eumenides*, by comparison with any other Attic tragedy, is its direct involvement with the political situation existing in Athens at the time when the play was first produced. Until the end of the episodes at Delphi, the *Oresteia*'s action is laid in the practically timeless world of heroic saga. From the moment (1. 235) at which the scene shifts to Athens, the drama homes in increasingly on the Athenian here and now. The Furies are made to appear, concurrently, less and less as insensate bloodhounds seeking the punishment of a matricide merely by instinctive reflex, and more and more as the upholders of an ancient tradition of family values, a tradition that to them represents justice, *dikē* (see their song in lines 490–565, and especially 508–16). It must be said, even perhaps at the cost of arousing a smile, that by the middle of the *Eumenides* the Furies are seen to be strict conservatives, in human as in cosmic politics. On the other hand, the Olympian representatives, first Apollo and then Athena, defend—the latter more moderately and intelligently than the former—a still perfectly recognizable liberal point of view: human and divine society can be changed by political means, and there may be times when this becomes necessary, even at great risk to inherited traditions of conduct.

The fundamental conflict in values represented by the two parties in the *Eumenides* has, of course, been a persistent feature of Western civilization ever since, and there have been (and will yet be, so long as that civilization endures) many times when it has shaken a social fabric to pieces, or come very close to doing so. One may think, for instance, of the sixteenth- and seventeenth-century wars of religion; or of the Vietnam years. But here above all, as we approach the *Eumenides,* it is pertinent to recall . . . the political and social transitions that were taking place during the last years of Aeschylus's life—the violent reform of the ancient court of Areopagus, the institution of the Periclean democracy (a process that was reaching its climax during the very year in which the *Oresteia* was first played), and the concurrent revolution in intellectual and religious, as well as political life. What makes this particular clash between the conservative and the liberal mentalities different is that it was the first such clash in recorded history—at least on this scale and with this variety of dimensions. The rift in Aeschylus's dramatic cosmos was paralleled by the rift in Aeschylus's city and perhaps—who knows?—the rift in his very soul and in the souls of his fellow citizens. The *Eumenides* seems to attempt both a diagnosis of and a remedy for what was then a new and fearsome disease of human society. That disease, now inveterate, remains fearsome; and Aeschylus's insights into it, at that historical moment when it first struck our society with the abrupt force of plague, may still reward our study.

But how, at this distance, can we penetrate to those insights? The difficulties are great. . . . The drama of Aeschylus is unique (at least in the Western world) in that, to the end, he worked in and through the language, the shapes, and the symbolism of the ancient mythology in all their dreamlike strangeness; and yet through that very medium he tried to come to grips with the great fifth-century transition from the very old ways of thinking to the very new. We cannot expect from that medium, as perhaps too many modern commentators and students have expected, a logical exposition of the problems and solutions. What we can reasonably expect—and what, I think, we get, above all in the *Eumenides*—is an almost absurdist drama, in which the events are superficially incongruous or incredible to the philosophically trained mind, but in which the symbolism pierces home to truth. One example of a scene composed in that mode, the recognition between Orestes and Electra, was singled out for discussion above. In the *Eumenides* we have before us an entire play so composed. Before considering its course, we may do well to recall some . . . words of Artaud. . . .

> Manikins, enormous masks, objects of strange proportions, will appear with the same sanction as verbal images. . . .
> The Theater of Cruelty will choose subjects and themes corresponding to the agitation and unrest characteristic of our epoch. . . . It will cause not only the recto but the verso of

the mind to play its part; the reality of imagination and dreams will appear there on an equal footing with life.

*Eumenides* falls into three main movements, of which the first (ll. 1–234) is set before the door of Apollo's temple at Delphi. A series of brief scenes expounds the contrast between the radiant Olympian god and the black, bestial creatures which have swarmed out of the depths of the earth into his sanctuary. The serenity of the Priestess's opening prayer to the gods and landscape of Delphi (significantly, in view of the play's outcome, it begins with Earth and ends with "Zeus the Highest") stands in shocking contrast to the second half of her speech, where she tries to describe the vision that awaited her after her solemn entrance into the temple at line 34. Her report makes it clear that for Orestes the light has once more failed, even Apollo's "undying light of fire." Even as he sits at the very center of Apollo-worship, his hands are still, magically, dripping with Clytaemnestra's blood, and he is encircled by sleeping female creatures whose horrific nature the priestess can only report in a breathless series of rejected comparisons: these things are women but not women, Gorgons but not Gorgons, Harpies but not Harpies. Something worse even than the worst horrors created by the ancient mythic imagination has crept out of the pit.

After the exit of the Priestess, the divine adversaries and their human protegés are brought in turn before our eyes. First Orestes enters from the temple accompanied by Apollo, who tells him that he must now wander over land and sea, pursued by the Furies, until he comes to Athens. There he is to embrace Athena's image, and there jurors, *dikastai,* will be found to try his case. Thus, says Apollo (ll. 82–83), "I shall find ways utterly to deliver you from these pains"; again we hear an echo of the phrase used by the Watchman at the opening of the trilogy. After the god and the man have left the scene, it is the turn of the female party. In one of his most superb imaginative strokes Aeschylus introduces the murdered Clytaemnestra, still showing the gashes that Orestes inflicted on her, not just as a ghost but as the dream of a ghost, angrily appealing to her patrons, the Furies, rousing them from the depths of their sleep. Here yet another motif that has persisted throughout the *Oresteia* seems to reach its climax; its first, muted introduction may be sought in the Watchman's insistence that *his* bed is not visited by dreams.

How this scene was staged is uncertain, but I would follow those who guess that the figure of the dream-ghost appears at the open door of the temple, calling to the Furies still unseen within, then vanishes as they awaken and make their way out one by one into the view of the spectators. However it was staged their epiphany must have been sensational. Characteristically, Aeschylus had built up the suspense and mystery by verbal means, step by step from Clytaemnestra's riddling threat in the *Libation-Bearers* (l. 924), through the vision seen by the crazed Orestes at the end of the same play, to the description by the bewildered Priestess as she reentered from the polluted shrine; now, and only now, appeared the visible reality. The story in the anonymous ancient Greek *Life of Aeschylus* that through this apparition the poet "so shocked the people that the children fainted away, and there were miscarriages," may not be literally true (for the *Life* is a late and reckless compilation from all kinds of sources, reliable and the reverse), but it seems very well invented on the basis of the text.

Now that the divine adversaries have been manifested separately, the time has arrived for their confrontation in the last of the scenes at Delphi (ll. 179–231), where the resplendent Apollo threatens the black and hideous Furies with his golden bow. This tableau may be said to mark the lowest point of despair in the *Oresteia;* both the vision and the words that accompany it indicate a hopeless and irreconcilable enmity between the opposed divine forces who for the present control events. Before passing on from that dread vision to the central movement of the *Eumenides* (ll. 235–777), we should pause to consider a question that is perhaps not asked often enough either in practical living or in the criticism of Aeschylus: *how are debates on vital issues actually won?* Between adversaries opposed on grounds of deeply felt principle, unfortunately for humanity, simple reasoning rarely seems to achieve much—no more than simple arithmetic can achieve in a debate on moral values, for instance. In such matters conversion to another's point of view, on the rare occasions when it occurs, is rather a process of *turning* (as is implied in the etymology of the word *conversion*), a turning of the total personality of each party toward that of the other in such a way as to reveal previously unrecognized compatible qualities; and this difficult process is apt to be induced by the heavy stress of changing events rather than by mere verbal persuasion.

It is through such a revolving of attributes on both sides that the apparently hopeless deadlock of the Delphi scenes is ultimately resolved. This technique (or this intuition into life's actual workings?) seems to be traceable in the other plays of Aeschylus's second group also. We have seen indications of a turning of the Danaids' character in the opposite sense, from fair to foul, in the *Suppliants* trilogy; and it may appear from our consideration of the Prometheus plays that the apparent contradictions in *Prometheus Bound* can best be explained—perhaps can *only* be explained—by the assumption that the characters of Prometheus and Zeus were also turned as the trilogy progressed. The *Eumenides,* however, provides the most easily studied case history of the process, because here alone it can be followed in its entirety. During its first stage, in the Delphi scenes, the Furies are characterized by all parties, including themselves, as bestial creatures actuated purely by lust for the sinner's blood. The imagery of animals is applied to them repeatedly; they are likened to snakes (l. 127), goats (l. 196), lions (l. 193), unnamed monsters which bloat themselves on human gore (ll. 183–84), and above all to blood-hounds (ll. 131–32). That bestial aspect is all that we are permitted to see in them during the Delphi scenes; and as for Apollo, it is all that he ever manages to see in them. As late in the play as line 664, long after the animal imagery has been dropped by every other speaker, Apollo, being deftly outwitted by them in argument at the trial, resorts to shouting at them: "Beasts hateful every way!" So long as he alone represents the Olympians in their dealings with the Furies, there is not the slightest chance of an agreement. He remains throughout an inflexible doctrinaire.

Change can come only at Athens, and with the intervention of Athens' goddess. From Delphi to Athens the scene abruptly shifts at line 235, and we enter the long central movement of the play. It comprises, in brief, the arrival of Orestes at Athena's temple, followed at a short interval by that of the pursuing Furies; his appeal for the goddess's protection; her arrival from afar, and her persuasion of both parties to submit their quarrel to her discretion; and, finally, the trial and acquittal of Orestes before a jury of Athenians. Before we approach the climax of this movement, the trial—the most surreal of all scenes in extant Aeschylus—it will be rewarding to consider the nature of Athena and her effect on the Furies. Unlike the Delphic Apollo but like her namesake city of Athens, Athena proves able and willing to understand both parties in the dispute, the female and the male, the old and the new. Of all the deities of Olympus she is best fitted to mediate between these parties, because, in accordance with a tradition that in part is at least as old as Homer, she partakes of the attributes of both sexes. Already in Homer she is at once a virgin and a mighty force in battle. She is patroness of the traditionally feminine art of weaving, yet also, in post-Homeric times, of the traditionally masculine arts of the potter and the sculptor, who in archaic and classical Greece, especially in Athens, loved to represent her in a guise utterly paradoxical not only to an ancient Greek but also to the peoples of most cultures until well into the twentieth century: as a slender, delicate woman fully equipped as a heavy-armed infantryman.

In the opening scene at Athens, before the arrival of Athena, the Furies continue to display the bestial aspect that they had displayed at Delphi: "it smiles at me, the reek of human blood," they cry at their first arrival, as like hounds they cast around for their victim, Orestes (l. 253; for other animal imagery applied by the Furies to themselves during this episode, compare ll. 264–67, 302, 305, 326). After that arrival there are no more hints of animality in the play, with the exception of that put into the mouth of Apollo at line 664. Athena's courteous opening words to them immediately set a new tone. Responding to her with equal courtesy and moderation, they quietly explain their function in the cosmos, which is now represented as the seeking out and punishment for familial murders; and they, as well as Orestes, agree to entrust the decision in their case to Athena. When she has listened to both parties, she announces (ll. 470–89) that in so difficult a case the only recourse is to a *trial*—a trial before a court of Athenian citizens.

At this point yet another of those verbal and moral ambiguities that have haunted the two earlier plays of the *Oresteia* begins to be resolved. So far in the trilogy we have heard many conflicting appeals by all parties to *dikē*, a word which up to now has been quite fairly translatable into English as "justice," in the contexts in which it has appeared. But "justice" is only one of a wide range of meanings that *dikē* may possess in Greek, and that—unfortunately for translators of the *Oresteia* and their readers—have to be rendered by a correspondingly wide range of different English words. Among those meanings, one that occurs with increasing frequency in the litigious democracy of fifth-century Athens is "trial." In the episode following this speech of Athena, a *dikē*, at last defined in this sense, will be enacted before the audience's eyes. Such an evolution from ambiguity toward definition, first in the word, finally in the visually manifested thing, will be familiar enough by this stage in our progress through the plays, but this instance seems outstandingly significant for the interpretation of the entire trilogy. Whatever the result of the forthcoming trial may turn out to be, we have at this point suddenly leapt forward from the era of the interminable human or even divine vendetta, in which each successive participant claims the sanction of his own *dikē* as "justice," to an era in which the body politic intervenes to decide once for all which claim may stand by means of *dikē* as "trial." And this leap from the primaeval past into the present (in some sense, not merely the present of Aeschylus and his contemporaries, but also our own) has been made possible by Athena and in her city, Athens.

Not surprisingly, it will be long before the Furies can accept this utterly unforeseen development. Even as Athena leaves to select a jury from the Athenian citizenry, they break into a song (ll. 490–565) in which they appeal throughout to *dikē*, but in its most ancient sense: that of a goddess, Justice personified. Her rights and theirs, they sing, are threatened by this new institution, a trial at law. If the matricide Orestes goes free as a result of it, henceforth no one, whether father or mother, will any longer be able to call on Justice or the Furies for vengeance. "The house of Justice is collapsing!" (l. 516), for no man will revere her if he is not held in check by fear of punishment. Then follows a very significant appeal, whether to the audience, to Athens, or to mankind is left unclear in the context:

> Do not accept the life of anarchy,
> Nor yet the life of tyranny!
> For to the middle way,
> In all things, God has granted victory!
> (ll. 526–30)

To state the drift of the song as a whole, there is a traditional morality (the Furies name it, or rather her, *Dikē*) that transcends the proceedings of any human law court, and society will fall apart if that morality is not enforced by an element of fear. On the other hand, the man who respects it may live prosperously and without constraints. Here is yet another gentle revolution in the character of the Furies. Contact with the intelligent and civilized patron goddess of Athens has brought out a side of them at which one could never have guessed while watching their earlier confrontation with the blustering Apollo. They remain determined to punish the matricide, but their motivation is no longer that of the bloodhound programmed solely to seek out and destroy. They justify their determination by a principle with which, so far as it goes, few thoughtful persons of any society in any era could disagree. Certainly Athena does not, as will be seen shortly.

After the end of that choral song, the imagined setting seems to change from Athena's temple and image on the Acropolis to the top of the low hill that lies just to the west of it, the Areopagus. This, of course, is the very place in which the Athenian court of Areopagus held its sessions in Aeschylus's day, as it had always done throughout the recorded history of the city. The dispute over the status of this court . . . was the focal point of the fierce constitutional struggle of the years ca. 463–458 B.C., which ended in the triumph of the new democracy under the leadership of Pericles. Until that crisis, the court had not only held jurisdiction over many areas of legal dispute but had also exercised very wide and not very clearly defined powers over the government of Athens in general. To the democrats, bent on securing a system that would allow direct participation of all the citizens in the executive magistracies, the legislative assembly, and the law courts, such an archaic and unrepresentative institution was plainly intolerable. They succeeded eventually, amid great factional violence, in stripping the Areopagus court of all its prerogatives except jurisdiction in homicide cases and a few politically insignificant ritual functions. Thus, in this trial scene, the action of the *Oresteia* has moved from far away heroic Argos to focus on the heart and center of the contemporary political struggle in Athens: a hill, and a court, that were the major symbols of that struggle. The atmosphere in the Theater of Dionysus, as this point gradually became clear, may well have been charged with lightning: what would the poet say—what *could* he say—that was not certain to outrage the convictions of about half his audience? It may perhaps be at this point that one begins fully to realize the majesty and the danger of the project that Aeschylus had undertaken in the *Oresteia:* a diagnosis of the political and spiritual ills both of the very ancient way of life and of the very new; to be followed, in the last few minutes of the trilogy, by a magnificent symbolic enactment in spectacle and music of the only cure.

Aeschylean surrealism reaches its acme in the trial scene. That a jury of human beings should sit to vote on a case that has divided the powers of Heaven and Earth, the attorneys for the prosecution being daughters of Night and nieces of Fate, while the defense counsel is a son of Zeus and his spokesman! It is fantastic; and yet at a different level the scene hits the deep truth of the intellectual, political, and religious crisis that was upon the Athenian of 458 B.C. He was moving fast into a world wherein, literally, *the onus of judging rests on the human being,* even when he must judge between gods. The arguments presented to the court by counsel are, simply considered as instruments of rational persuasion, scarcely more plausible than the setting of the trial as a whole (how could they be?). It is no wonder that neither counsel in fact proves to have brought over the jury to his side, but that the eventual vote is split down the middle. On the other hand, their arguments do achieve what was surely the dramatist's intended effect: to bring out at their most vivid the natures of the contestants and of the issues involved in the struggle, whether on the divine level or on the contemporary political one.

With admirable evenhandedness, Aeschylus assigns far readier legal wits to the Furies than he does to their powerful opponents. They drive first Orestes (ll. 604–13) and then even Apollo (ll. 640–56) into apparent logical impasses. Apollo only extracts himself by abruptly switching his attack to their fundamental premise (expressed concisely at lines 602–8): that the guilt of matricide outweighs the guilt of husband-murder because the former violates blood ties, the latter does not; to the Furies it is the female, not the male, who creates the child and thus guarantees the perpetuation of the clan. And it is with that primaeval and natural social unit, the clan, and its values, that they are concerned, not with any later and artificial unit such as a city. Apollo's counterblast to that premise may well have knocked many of the audience flat, and has continued to dumbfound many of Aeschylus's critics down to the present day (ll. 658–61): "She who is called the mother of a child is not its creator, but only the nurse of the newly sown seed. The creator is he who begets; *she* keeps safe the plant for him, as a stranger for a stranger, granted God brings it to no harm." As a material witness to the accuracy of this statement, Apollo calls in very flattering language on Athena herself, who was born of no female but sprang perfect from the head of Zeus. He concludes the presentation of his case with a promise to ensure the future greatness of Athens, in part through Orestes who, if acquitted, will join his city of Argos in eternal alliance with Athena's city.

This, at first hearing, very surprising speech only begins to make sense in the dramatic and political context as one comes to realize that Apollo is here speaking with the voice of the liberal reformists of contemporary Athens. His promise of a permanent Argive alliance (which Orestes repeats and amplifies in his postacquittal speech, lines 762–74) can scarcely be anything but a direct reference to the total reversal of Athenian foreign policy that the Periclean party brought about concurrently with their central domestic enterprise, the reform of the Areopagus. Under the unreformed Areopagite regime that foreign policy had been firmly anchored on an alliance with Sparta, the most conservative, politically and intellectually, of the Greek city-states. The democrats abruptly broke off the Spartan alliance and allied Athens with Sparta's traditionally bitter enemy, Argos, which at that time seems also to have been governed under a form of democracy. Apollo's argument against the participation of the female in the process of conception seems equally to allude to a heated contemporary controversy, but in this case a scientific one. A number of Greek philosopher-scientists are known to have been debating this question during the middle decades of the fifth century, among them Pericles' friend Anaxagoras. The evidence for the position that Anaxagoras took on it is somewhat confused, but our most reliable witness, Aristotle, implies that he argued, as Apollo does here, that the male's semen was the sole source of human life and that the womb merely constituted a receptacle for its growth. Thus the champion of the male defendant in the trial scene of the *Eumenides* is now seen to favor views which the audience could scarcely have failed to identify, respectively, with those of the newly triumphant democratic reformers and of the advanced thinkers in the circle of Pericles.

After that speech both parties rest their cases. Before the crucial vote is taken, however, Athena intervenes in the proceedings with a long speech (ll. 681–710) in which she proclaims that this court, summoned ad hoc for the trial of Orestes, is to exist henceforth forever in her city as the court of Areopagus. Day and night alike, she foretells, this court will keep watch over Athens, and the fear of it will restrain the citizens from unjust action. In this context she adds some general advice on political conduct

> I urge my citizens to revere and keep
> That state which is not anarchy or tyranny,
> And not to expel all terror from the city.
> What human being is just when freed from fear?
> (ll. 696–99)

Notable in these lines is the community of feeling between Athena and the Furies, who have voiced the same opinions in very nearly the same words at lines 517–30. The speech as a whole, indeed, seems designed to conciliate those conservative Athenians—the human counterparts of the Furies—to whom the Areopagus had always been the most important and most stable element in the governing of the city. In this Athena's diplomacy is exquisite. Her praise of the Areopagus is unbounded, yet the only function of the court she mentions specifically is that for which she has summoned it on the present occasion: a homicide trial. And this, as we saw, was the one significant function the reforming democrats had left to it anyway.

While the silent Areopagite jurors cast their voting-pebbles into the ballot urns (ll. 711ff.), Apollo and the Furies exchange pointed insults. As the voting draws to a close, Athena announces that she too will cast her pebble—in favor of Orestes, since she belongs to the male side, the side of her sole parent, Zeus; even should the human votes be equal, therefore, Orestes will win his case. The count of votes begins, while the anxious litigants exclaim, in the contrasting imagery that has pervaded the *Oresteia* from its beginning.

> ORESTES: Shining Apollo, how will the trial be judged?
> CHORUS: Black mother Night, do you behold this thing?
> ORESTES: Now shall I die by the noose—or see the light!
> (ll. 744–46)

The votes prove, in fact, to be even; the human beings have been no less in favor of the female/dark than of the male/light. Orestes escapes punishment for his matricide by a hair's breadth, through that gentle pressure laid on the scales by the patron deity of Athens, who is something between the male and the female, who, like her citizens in 458 B.C., has her being in the "no-man's-land of dark and light." (That enigmatic Aeschylean phrase, which seemed the appropriate epigraph for this final chapter, comes from the opening chorus of the *Libation-Bearers,* line 63).

And so Orestes goes free, having found that deliverance from his pains which Apollo had promised him at the beginning of the play, and having beheld at last a light that does not delude. The human family feud is done with. Apollo, too, has left the scene by now, although at what point we do not know. In our text of the play his last speech is at lines 748–51, where he bids the jurors count the votes. The *Oresteia* as a whole represents Apollo as an unsympathetic being, from *Agamemnon* lines 1202–12, where Cassandra relates how he punished her for refusing to make love to her ("What?" says the Chorus there, "A *God* struck by desire?"), through the description of his fantastic threats to Orestes should he fail to carry out the matricide in the *Libation-Bearers* lines 269–96, to his onstage behavior in the *Eumenides.* He is an extremist in all his relationships with the feminine principle; it is surely significant that the last mythological exploit of his of which we hear in the *Eumenides* (ll. 723–28) is the bizarre tale of how he cheated those most august of pre-Olympian goddesses, the Fates, by making them drunk. But neither the finale of the *Oresteia* nor the Athens of 458 B.C., of which it is an ideal projection, have any place for extremists. Apollo leaves without farewells.

As we enter the third and last movement of the *Eumenides* (ll. 778–1047) there remain in the *orchēstra* the threatening black rectangle formed by the Chorus, and Athena, perhaps in front of the *skēnē* and facing them; behind her we may well imagine the still silent jurors of the Areopagus, representing the people of her city. It at once appears that the acquittal of Orestes, however happy for him, has raised terrible problems, in its turn, for the city and the cosmos. The Furies break into a frantic song and dance of hate against the "younger Gods," the Olympians, and against the land and people of Athens. Here we must revert for the last time in this account of the *Eumenides* to the phenomenon that I have called the "turning" of the Furies' character. We have seen how they appeared in the early scenes of the play as utterly revolting creatures, characterized primarily as animals in form and instinct. So they remained as long as they were confronted only by the divine and human males Apollo and Orestes. With the epiphany of the androgynous Athena, their animal characteristics have faded out and they have taken on the aspect of highly articulate conservatives, upholding the perpetuation of immemorially ancient traditions in both cosmic and human affairs, with a ready and sometimes even entertaining wit. And so they have remained, on the whole, until the acquittal of Orestes. Nevertheless, as early as their first encounter with Athena there has been a hint of yet another aspect of their nature. Even as she decides to prepare for a trial, Athena is apprehensive of this aspect (ll. 477–79): supposing their case is defeated, "hereafter poison shall proceed out of their angry spirits, poison falling on the land as an unbearable, unending plague." As the crisis of the trial approaches, the Furies do in fact utter threats against the Attic landscape (ll. 711 and 720), and Apollo taunts them in these words (ll. 729–30): "In a moment you are going to lose this case and vomit up that poison of yours, but it won't do your enemies the slightest harm!"

This new aspect that the Furies are gradually turning toward the audience is, like the former ones, perfectly congruous with their fundamental character as female earthdwellers. As we saw early in this book, Earth not merely hides within her the dead and the places of judgment, but she is also responsible for the fertility of the humans, animals, and plants that exist on her surface. The Furies are now emerging as fertility goddesses, with the power to blight or prosper the life of nature at their will. In the raging song with which they open the third movement of the play, they threaten to turn the destructive side of this power against Athens, in horrific words that might equally apply to the effects of nuclear radiation:

> Shooting from my very heart
> Poison, poison for my pain;
> It shall drip upon your land
> Unbearable, and from it rise

> Canker blasting leaf and child
> (HEAR ME, JUSTICE!)
> Canker racing through the plain!
> (ll. 782–86)

In the ensuing interchange, lasting until line 919, Athena takes hold of this fertility function of the Furies and works to convert it from its destructive to its creative aspect. As she talks to them, their wild outbursts of song and dance grow shorter, until at line 892 they are calm enough at last to engage with her in spoken line-for-line dialogue. Athena meets their rage with gentle persuasion, with promises of an honored place in the human and divine community of Athens, and, at one point (ll. 826–29), with a delicate reminder that she has direct access to Zeus's thunderbolt arsenal. (In this situation, too, the principle that she shares with the Furies holds good, as it continues to hold good in most compacts, whether between individuals or between nations: there must be an element of fear, but it must not be the sole element.) Toward the end of the line-by-line dialogue they tentatively begin to yield to Athena's offer of an honored home in a city whose future promises ever more honor. What hymn, they ask her, would she have them sing over her land? Athena's answer to that begins with language (ll. 903–9) that might remind one of Aphrodite's language in her speech on the marriage of Earth and Sky, in the *Danaides:*

> Blessings to suit a blameless victory!
> Blessings from the earth and from the ocean waters
> And from the sky! Pray that the airy winds
> Breathe sunshine as they march across the land,
> That the yields of earth and cattle never fail
> My citizens, but thrive to overflowing,
> That human seed in safety ever grow!

She concludes by asking the Furies also to foster piety and justice in her city (in this, appealing to the different aspect of themselves which they have revealed in the middle movement of the play) and by predicting a glorious future for Athens in external wars.

As Athena ends this speech, the Furies break into a joyous song and dance, each stanza of which is answered in an equally joyous recitative passage by Athena. In the course of this marvelous antiphony the Furies happily accept residency (*metoikia*) in Athens, calling down on the city all the blessings that Athena has asked for, and more besides. They appeal to the Fates, as "spirits of right law" (l. 963), to grant health and happy marriage to the Athenian youth. They pray that "the thunder of Strife, who cannot eat her fill of evils, may never be heard in this city" (ll. 976–78), and that there be no "dooms of murder answering murder" (l. 982), but that the citizens "may exchange joys for joys among each other in a spirit of mutual love, and may hate the enemy as with one mind, for this is the way to cure many of the evils among humanity" (ll. 984–87). Toward the end of the singing a processsion of citizens is forming under Athena's orders, and after the last exultant stanza dies away she proclaims that this procession is to escort the Furies with the glare of torchlight to their new home, a cave beneath the earth (presumably identifiable with the shrine at the foot of the Areopagus hill, which was shown as theirs to visitors in later antiquity). This speech of Athena's (ll. 1021–31), as we now have it in the few manuscripts of the *Eumenides,* has almost certainly been mutilated in transmission. Two ancient accounts of the play mention that "after Athena had calmed the Furies" she gave them a new name, Eumenides—that is, the Kindly Ones. No such passage occurs in the text of the *Eumenides* which has survived in the manuscripts, but the very title of the play proves that it must once have existed, and the obvious place for it would be here. Such a formal reversal in the Chorus's name would not merely be a fitting culmination to the reversal in its feelings wrought by Athena; it would also fit very well with the two magnificent visual gestures that either accompanied this speech or took place immediately after it. At lines 1025–26 Athena orders:

> By draping them in cloaks of crimson dye
> Honor them, and let the light of fire move on!

Thus, in these final moments of the trilogy, the black rectangle that has dominated the dancing floor since the mourning chorus entered at the beginning of the *Libation-Bearers* turns to crimson, as attendants throw the cloaks round the shoulders of the Kindly Ones. The symbolism of this gesture may be more complex than appears at first sight. It is known that at Athens' greatest civic festival, the Panathenaea, the resident aliens (*metoikoi*) marched in the procession wearing crimson robes; thus the new dress visually clinches the Kindly Ones' acceptance of their new status of *metoikia* in the city. But this is also the third occasion in the trilogy on which the theater has been brightened by wide expanses of colored drapery. The former two were the Tapestry Scene of *Agamemnon,* in which the king walked on purple to his death, and the scene in the *Libation-Bearers* where Orestes, standing over the dead bodies of his mother and Aegisthus, had the attendants hold up the bloody murder-robe. Like so many other images in the *Oresteia,* verbal and visual, the colored cloth that had been a symbol of dread becomes, at the end, a symbol of joy and reconciliation.

The final visual gesture is the great flaring of torches as the procession, headed by Athena (ll. 1003–5), moves off to lead the Kindly Ones, "children of Night no more her children" (l. 1034) toward their new home under the earth. Here an image that has recurred ambiguously in words throughout the trilogy, from the prologue of *Agamemnon* onward, is finally made visible and given a definitive and joyful meaning. The retreat of the light back toward the darkness of the cave of the Kindly Ones signifies the end of the feud between male and female (in both their literal and figurative senses) in the family, the city, and the cosmos. As the escorting citizens sing in the very last words of the *Eumenides,* the two ultimate principals in that feud, the Father of the Olympians and the pre-Olympian Goddess of Destiny, are now at one:

> Thus Zeus the all seeing
> And Fate have come together;
> Cry out for joy at this our song!

The torchlights, the crimson robes, disappear through the side entrance; the tragedy (or comedy, or masque, or dream?) is ended. The *Oresteia* production, however, is not. After this the audience sits back and smiles over the satyr-play *Proteus,* which tells of Agamemnon's brother Menelaus, marooned among the merry satyrs on an islet near the Egyptian coast, to which he has strayed during his voyage home from the pitiless sack of Troy—so long ago, it now seems.

# Chronology

| | |
|---|---|
| ca. 525 B.C.E. | Aeschylus born at Eleusis. |
| 499–96 | Aeschylus first competes in the drama festival of the Great Dionysia in Athens. |
| 490 | Fights in the battle of Marathon. |
| 484 | Wins first dramatic competition. |
| 472 | Wins first prize for the tetralogy that includes *Persians*. (The other plays are now lost.) |
| 472–68 | Aeschylus travels to Sicily. *Women of Aetne* produced. |
| 468 | Sophocles, in his first competition, defeats Aeschylus. |
| 467 | *Seven against Thebes* produced. Aeschylus wins first prize. |
| ca. 463 | *Suppliants* produced. Aeschylus wins first prize. |
| 458 | *Oresteia* produced. Aeschylus wins first prize. |
| 456 | Aeschylus travels again to Sicily and dies there, at Gela. |

# Contributors

HAROLD BLOOM, Sterling Professor of the Humanities at Yale University, is the author of *The Anxiety of Influence, Poetry and Repression,* and many other volumes of literary criticism. His forthcoming study, *Freud: Transference and Authority,* attempts a full-scale reading of all of Freud's major writings. A MacArthur Prize Fellow, he is general editor of five series of literary criticism published by Chelsea House. During 1987–88, he served as Charles Eliot Norton Professor of Poetry at Harvard University.

JOHN JONES is a Fellow of New College, Oxford. His books include studies of Wordsworth, Keats, Dostoevsky, and Dickens.

ANNE LEBECK was Associate Professor of Classics at Amherst College. She is the author of a number of articles including "The Central Myth of Plato's *Phaedrus.*"

FROMA I. ZEITLIN is Professor of Classics at Princeton University and the author of several articles on Aeschylus and other classical subjects.

PIERRE VIDAL-NAQUET is Director of Studies and Professor of Sociology at the Ecole Pratique des Hautes Etudes, Paris, and the coauthor of *Economic and Social History of Ancient Greece.*

W. B. STANFORD is Chancellor of the University of Dublin, where he was previously Regius Professor of Greek. He is the author of *Ambiguity in Greek Literature, Aeschylus in His Style,* and many other classical studies.

JOHN HERINGTON is Talcott Professor of Greek at Yale University. His books include *Poetry into Drama: Early Tragedy and the Greek Poetic Tradition.*

# Bibliography

Betensky, A. "Aeschylus' *Oresteia:* The Power of Clytemnestra." *Ramus* 7 (1978): 11–25.

Burke, Kenneth. "Form and Persecution in the *Oresteia.*" *Sewanee Review* 60 (1952): 377–96.

Burkert, Walter. "Greek Tragedy and Sacrificial Ritual." *Greek, Roman and Byzantine Studies* 7 (1966): 87–121.

———. "A Note on Aeschylus' *Choephori* 205ff." *Classical Quarterly* 57 (1963): 177.

Caldwell, R. S. "The Pattern of Aeschylean Tragedy." *Transactions of the American Philological Association* 101 (1970): 77–94.

Conacher, D. J. "Interaction Between Chorus and Characters in the *Oresteia.*" *American Journal of Philology* 95 (1974): 323–43.

Dawe, R. D. "Inconsistency of Plot and Character in Aeschylus." *Proceedings of the Cambridge Philological Society* 9 (1963): 21–62.

de Romilly, Jacqueline. *Time in Greek Tragedy.* Ithaca, N.Y.: Cornell University Press, 1968.

Dodds, E. R. "Morals and Politics in the *Oresteia.*" In *The Ancient Concept of Progress and Other Essays,* 45–63. Oxford: Oxford University Press, 1973.

Dover, K. J. "The Political Aspect of the *Eumenides.*" *Journal of Hellenic Studies* 77 (1957): 230–37.

Easterling, P. E. "Presentation of Character in Aeschylus." *Greece and Rome* 20 (1973): 3–18.

Edwards, Mark. "Agamemnon's Decision: Freedom and Folly in Aeschylus." *California Studies in Classical Antiquity* 10 (1977): 17–38.

Else, G. *The Origin and Early Form of Greek Tragedy.* Cambridge: Harvard University Press, 1965.

———. "Ritual and Drama in Aeschylean Tragedy." *Illinois Classical Studies* 2 (1977): 70–87.

Finley, John H. *Pindar and Aeschylus.* Cambridge: Harvard University Press, 1955.

Fontenrose, J. "Men and Gods in the *Oresteia.*" *Transactions of the American Philological Society* 102 (1971): 71–109.

Gagarin, M. *Aeschylean Drama.* Berkeley and Los Angeles: University of California Press, 1970.

Gantz, T. "Inherited Guilt in Aeschylus." *Classical Journal* 78 (1982): 1–23.

Goheen, R. F. "Three Studies in the *Oresteia.*" *American Journal of Philology* 76 (1955): 113–37.

Hammond, N. G. L. "Personal Freedom and its Limitations in the *Oresteia*." *Journal of Hellenic Studies* 85 (1965): 42–55.

Herrington, C. J. "The Influence of Old Comedy on Aeschylus' Later Trilogies." *Transactions of the American Philological Society* 94 (1963): 113–25.

Hester, D. A. "The Casting Vote." *American Journal of Philology* 102 (1981): 265–74.

Higgins, W. E. "Double-Dealing Ares in the *Oresteia*." *Classical Philology* 73 (1978): 24–35.

Ireland, S. "Stichomythia in Aeschylus." *Hermes* 102 (1974): 509–24.

Kells, J. H. "Aeschylus' *Eumenides* 213–14 and Athenian Marriage." *Classical Philology* 56 (1961): 169–73.

Kitto, H. D. F. *Poiesis*. Berkeley: University of California Press, 1966.

———. *Form and Meaning in Drama*. London: Methuen, 1956.

Knox, Bernard M. W. "The Lion in the House." *Classical Philology* 47 (1952): 17–25.

Kramer, F. R. "The Altar of Right: Reality and Power in Aeschylus." *Classical Journal* 56 (1960): 33–38.

Kuhns, Richard. *The House, the City and the Judge: The Growth of Moral Awareness in the Oresteia*. Indianapolis: Bobbs-Merrill, 1962.

Lawrence, S. E. "Artemis in the *Agamemnon*." *American Journal of Philology* 97 (1976): 97–110.

Leary, D. M. "The Role of Cassandra in the *Agamemnon* of Aeschylus." *Bulletin of John Rylands Library* 52 (1969): 144–77.

———. "The Representation of the Trojan War in Aeschylus' *Agamemnon*." *American Journal of Philology* 95 (1974): 1–23.

Lebeck, Anne. "The First Stasimon of Aeschylus' *Choephori*: Myth and Mirror Image." *Classical Philology* 62 (1967): 182–84.

Lesky, Albin. "Decision and Responsibility in the Tragedy of Aeschylus." *Journal of Hellenic Studies* 86 (1966): 78–86.

Lloyd-Jones, Hugh. "The Guilt of Agamemnon." *Classical Quarterly* 12 (1962): 187–99.

———. "Zeus in Aeschylus." *Journal of Hellenic Studies* 76 (1956): 55–67.

Mejer, J. "Recognising What, When and Why: The Recognition Scenes in Aeschylus' *Choephori*." In *Hellenic Studies Presented to Bernard M. W. Knox*, edited by G. W. Bowersock, et al., 115–21. Berlin: de Gruyter.

Moritz, H. E. "Refrain in Aeschylus: Literary Adaptation of Traditional Form." *Classical Philology* 74 (1979): 187–213.

Otis, B. *Cosmos and Tragedy: An Essay on the Meaning of Aeschylus*. Chapel Hill: University of North Carolina Press, 1981.

Peradotto, John J. "Some Patterns of Nature Imagery in the *Oresteia*." *American Journal of Philology* 85 (1964): 378–93.

Podlecki, A. J. *The Political Background of Aeschylean Tragedy*. Ann Arbor: University of Michigan Press, 1966.

Rabinowitz, N. S. "From Force to Persuasion: Aeschylus' *Oresteia* as Cosmogonic Myth." *Ramus* 10 (1981): 159–91.

Reeves, C. J. "The Parados of the *Agamemnon*." *Classical Journal* 55 (1960): 165–71.

Rosenmeyer, Thomas G. "Gorgias, Aeschylus and *Apatē*." *American Journal of Philology* 76 (1955): 225–60.

————. *The Art of Aeschylus*. Berkeley: University of California Press, 1982.

Schein, S. "The Cassandra Scene in Aeschylus' *Choephori*." *Greece and Rome* 29 (1982): 11–16.

Stinton, Thomas. "The First Stasimon of Aeschylus' *Choephori*." *Classical Quarterly* 29 (1979): 252–62.

Taplin, Oliver. "Aeschylean Silences and Silences in Aeschylus." *Harvard Studies in Classical Philology* 76 (1972): 57–67.

————. *The Stagecraft of Aeschylus*. Oxford: Oxford University Press, 1977.

Tarkow, T. A. "Electra's Role in the Opening Scene of the *Choephori*." *Eranos* 77 (1979): 11–21.

Thomson, George. *Aeschylus and Athens*. London: Lawrence & Wishart, 1941.

Vellacott, P. "Has Good Prevailed? A Further Study of the *Oresteia*." *Harvard Studies in Classical Philology* 81 (1977): 113–22.

Vickers, Brian. *Towards Greek Tragedy*. London: Longman, 1973.

Winnington-Ingram, R. P. *Studies in Aeschylus*. Cambridge: Cambridge University Press, 1983.

Zeitlin, Froma I. "The Motif of the Corrupted Sacrifice in Aeschylus' *Oresteia*." *Transactions of the American Philological Association* 96 (1965): 463–508.

# Acknowledgments

"The House of Atreus" by John Jones from *On Aristotle and Greek Tragedy* by John Jones, © 1962 by John Jones. Reprinted by permission of Chatto & Windus Ltd.

"The Commos in the *Libation-Bearers*" (originally entitled "The Commos") by Anne Lebeck from The Oresteia: *A Study in Language and Structure* by Anne Lebeck, © 1971 by the Trustees for Harvard University, Center for Hellenic Studies, Washington, D.C. Reprinted by permission of Harvard University Press.

"The Dynamics of Misogyny: Myth and Mythmaking in the *Oresteia*" by Froma I. Zeitlin from *Arethusa* 2: "Women in the Ancient World" (1978), © 1978 by the Department of Classics, State University of New York at Buffalo. Reprinted by permission.

"Hunting and Sacrifice in Aeschylus's *Oresteia*" by Pierre Vidal-Naquet from *Tragedy and Myth in Ancient Greece* by Pierre Vidal-Naquet, translated by Janet Lloyd, © 1981 by the Harvester Press Ltd. Reprinted by permission.

"The Tragic Emotions in the *Oresteia*" by W. B. Stanford from *Greek Tragedy and the Emotions* by W. B. Stanford, © 1983 by W. B. Stanford. Reprinted by permission of Routledge & Kegan Paul Ltd.

"No-Man's-Land of Dark and Light" by John Herington from *Aeschylus* by John Herington, © 1986 by Yale University. Reprinted by permission of Yale University Press.

# Index